THE
GAME OF SQUASH

EUSTACE MILES, M.A.,
OF KING'S COLLEGE, CAMBRIDGE

Late Hon. Secretary to the Cambridge University Racquet Fives, and Squash Club, and a Governor of the Tuxedo Tennis and Racquet Club; Amateur Tennis Champion of England and the United States, Amateur Racquet Champion United States and Canada, Winner Open Competition in Amateur Racquet Championship of England

Author of

Lessons in "Lawn-Tennis," "The Training of the Body," "Muscle, Brain, and Diet," etc.

Dedicated
to
ROBERT BACON, ESQ.
THE HON. CECIL BARING
J. MACDONOUGH, ESQ.
HENRY W. POOR, ESQ.
T. SUFFERN TAILER, ESQ.
MY FELLOW GOVERNORS
OF THE
TUXEDO TENNIS AND RACQUET CLUB

Table of Contents

	PAGE
Preface.	v
Introduction. Merits of the Game of Squash	xiv

CHAPTER

1	The Court and Implements Described, with Suggestions	1
2	The Game and its Rules	21
3	Difficulties and Faults of Players	30
4	The Holding of the Racket	36
5	Forehand Position and Stroke	43
6	Backhand Position and Stroke	52
7	Positions and Movements before and after Strokes	58
8	Practice Outside the Court	65
9	Practice Inside the Court	81
10	The Game Itself	90
11	Handicaps	98
12	General Hints	106

ILLUSTRATIONS

	PAGE
12 How to Move towards a Ball...............	63
13 Turning on the Hips: (a) to the Right; (b) to the Left............................	71, 72
14 (a) and (b) A Wrist-Exercise	73, 74
15 Position in Waiting for a Ball off the Back-wall	85
16 Position before the Forehand Service........	86
17 Position before the Backhand Service........	88

PREFACE

How ought I to hold my racket? How ought I to stand before I make a Backhand stroke, and while I make it? How ought I to move during the stroke? What ought I to do afterwards? How can I practise, when I am busy all day? How can I improve my game and correct my faults? Why have I failed to improve? How can I keep in training, leading a sedentary life as I do? What is the best size, the best material, the best colour for a Court? What are the best rackets and balls? What are the rules of Squash? These are a few of the questions which are constantly being asked but which no book has answered; and these are a few of the questions which this book attempts to answer. And with the answers it will give the reasons for these answers: for Americans especially love to know the reason for everything.

For example, the learner is not only told to hold his racket with its head up, like a Hand-mirror, before he begins the stroke; he is also told the reason, viz. that thus he protects his head and has the racket nearly ready for the downward swing.

Again, when the learner is told how to stand before he makes a Backhand stroke, viz. to stand alert on his toes or on the balls of his feet, with his racket up, and then to move into the sideways-position (Ill. 11), with his left shoulder back, and so on, he is also told that to be alert on his toes will save time, that the sideways-position will give him a long free swing, as if he were a clock and his arm and racket were the clock's pendulum, and that the left shoulder, being back, will not be in the way of the swing and will actually help it, as in Golf.

But there is no need to multiply instances here. The answers to these and other questions will be found in the book itself. Here I need only say how I answer one more of them, viz. "Why have I failed to improve?"

I have tried to show (on p. 32 foll.) that one single correct stroke is not a simple movement, an indivisible unity, but a complex movement, a whole consisting of many parts and divisible into these parts. A correct stroke is, in fact, a correct combination of many correct parts.

One of the answers may therefore be encouraging to the player: "You may have failed to improve, chiefly because you were

PREFACE

doing some one or more of these parts incorrectly."

"How, then, can I practise and correct the stroke?" You can correct it part by part: as soon as you have found out what the parts are (see p. 48) you can begin to acquire them correctly one by one; if you are busy all day, you can acquire these parts quite easily just after you get up and just before you go to bed. The Exercises, most of which are very healthy, can be done at odd moments when there is nothing else to do, or at intervals between hours of work.

If you object that this will never teach you to play, then I ask how you learned to play the piano? Did you not first learn how to sit, how to hold the wrist, how to move the fingers, and so on? Or did you begin with a piece by Brahms?

Squash has no literature of its own: I believe that this is the first book on the game. In fact, till 1899, I had never seen an article on Squash, or even a report of a Match.

Nor has the game a large and interesting history, as Tennis (Court-Tennis) has. Until the present year, when a Cup was offered for the Amateur Championship of America at Tuxedo, there has not been a Squash-Championship, and there have been comparatively

St. Agnes Free Library
and
Reading Room.

few Squash-competitions. The game has no professionals devoted solely to it.

And yet the game is played and enjoyed by thousands of people in various parts of the world. In England the Universities and large Schools have their Courts constantly used; in America as well as in England many private houses have their Courts; and so have many of the Athletic Clubs in America. There is now a Court at Pau, and I hear that it is most popular.

Nor is Squash merely a game that is played by a number of people who cannot play anything else. It is played keenly by some of the very best athletes and sportsmen in the world. My great friend, Mr. George Richmond Fearing, Jr., has been one of the best all-round athletes in the world, and is a fine player of Squash.

In fact, Squash has a great future before it; and my intention in writing this book is not only to offer hints to players, to give reasons for these hints, and to answer objections, but also to point out the many advantages of the game, and the important place of the game in American as well as English life.

For Squash is very healthy exercise as well as cheap exercise, and it does not take up much time; and in Squash it is easy to reach the stage at which one can thoroughly enjoy the

PREFACE

game. For the game is easy and simple up to a certain point, as opposed to Tennis (Court-Tennis), which is generally found to be difficult up to a certain point. Squash is popular with all sorts of players, ladies, boys, elderly men, business-men, and brain-workers generally. For the latter it has a unique value, since it can be played (as it is in New York, Boston, and Tuxedo) by electric light.

At any time of the year, in any kind of weather, as well as at any time in the day, Squash is possible. America sadly needs winter games: Gymnastics will never do for a nation what games can hardly fail to do. And Squash is for the above reasons as well as for others an ideal winter game.

Besides this, as we shall see, it has a social value.

Squash is a good foundation for other games, and especially for Tennis (Court-Tennis) and Racquets and even Lawn Tennis: I consider it to be an indispensable preparation for the first two games. It is also a great help for Golf and Cricket, if it be learnt properly; indeed, it includes many of the fundamental movements of quite a large number of games and exercises.

I said if it be learnt properly, and this is an important proviso. If the learner gets a general idea of the game and the strokes, and then analyses and divides up the strokes into parts, and then practises these parts one by one, correctly and with constant repetition, and then combines these parts together, he will have thereby acquired a general method by which he can learn any form of exercise; or indeed, it may be, any subject.

These are among the chief reasons (for others, see the Introduction), why I have urged the building of Squash-Courts everywhere, by private individuals (p. 13), and by Schools, Universities, and Clubs. I have also suggested what seem to be the best dimensions, materials, colours, rackets, balls, and so on, and the various Rules of the game.

For Squash has different sets of rules, which give the game great variety. Further variety can be insured by the use of the Handicaps, on which I have written a special Chapter. The Science of Handicaps has yet to become an integral part of nearly every form of Athletics, if not of every form. It is essential, however, that the Handicap should improve the game of both players, and not compel the stronger to play the safety pat-ball game, and the weaker to 'force' the game by rash strokes or to wait till his opponent beats himself.

Some of the ideas of this book have appeared or will appear elsewhere, e. g. in an

PREFACE

article on "Sport and Athletics and the British Empire" (for Kegan Paul's 'British Empire' Series), in 'Lessons in Lawn-Tennis' (Upcott Gill), and "The Training of the Body" (Sonnenschein and Co.). But in these writings the ideas were not applied to Squash in particular; they will be applied to the other Ball-games in a larger volume which will be published later on.

I was originally led to adopt the 'Part-by-part' System of learning games owing to some excellent criticisms of my faults as a Racquet player. These criticisms were made by the great Racquet coach of Wellington College, Mr. Smale. He mentioned so many faults that I began to see that the only way to correct them was to correct them one by one. My grip was wrong, my wrist-position was wrong, my racket-head was held wrongly, my feet were in the wrong position, my shoulders were wrong, and so on. I thought it best to devise special Exercises, some of which I give in this book. At first they produced little effect, but soon I began to improve steadily; and I have been improving steadily ever since.

The Exercises I have altered from time to time, adapting them to various games, and correcting their errors, partly by watching the play of, or by listening to the opinions of, such experts as Tom Pettitt, Peter Latham, Robert Moore, T. P. Burke, and Messrs. H. S. Mahony, W. A. Briscoe, and some of the American Amateur players; and partly by reading various books on Ball-games.

The Diagrams I have tried to make as simple as possible: the Photos have been taken from behind, since a front view of a player is almost useless as a model: everything is the wrong way round for purposes of imitation. I might have given many more Diagrams and Photos, but these I shall reserve for the larger work. For this also I shall reserve many hints on play in general, and on the double game in particular: the double at Squash is very seldom played.

These and other details I have been obliged to omit for want of space, and also because in suggesting new ideas it is necessary to repeat them and to justify them and to lay emphasis on them by throwing subordinate ideas into the back-ground or by leaving them out altogether.

I shall be very grateful to any one who will point out any errors either in the general system which I offer or in my application of it to Squash in particular. But it is chiefly the general system and general principles which I shall recommend to the learner's notice: I

PREFACE

would rather try to give him the foundations of a good sound game of Squash, and succeed in this, than try to train him to a style of perfectly beautiful grace and finish and—be nearly sure to fail.

TUXEDO CLUB,
Tuxedo Park,
New York.

March, 1900.

INTRODUCTION

MERITS OF THE GAME OF SQUASH

So far as I am aware, no one has yet written in praise of Squash: to thousands the very name is unknown. It is high time for the game to receive a part of its due.

There are few who would claim that Squash is a perfect form of exercise, and there are some who would go so far as to deny that it has any great merit. They say that it is monotonous and wanting in variety; that it needs very little skill; that it is a selfish game, each player playing for himself alone and not for his side or for his team; and that it has to be played indoors.

These objections are quite sound up to a certain point; but they are not unanswerable. Let us see what can be said on the other side; and let us not forget that the game is at present undeveloped and is still growing. When it has lived and flourished as long as other games, then experience, the great teacher, will have taught it how to improve.

The objection that Squash is monotonous and wanting in variety would not hold good if

INTRODUCTION

the different games of Squash (Chapter II) were studied and practised, together with the different kinds of Handicaps (Chapter XI). Though Squash has not as much variety as Tennis (Court-Tennis), it yet has considerably more than appears at first sight. Like the game of Draughts, it has points in it which do not occur to the casual eye.

That Squash needs very little skill is quite a mistaken notion; in Chapters VII and VIII, we shall see that even the Foot-movements, which the game requires, are very complex in themselves, to say nothing of the use of the large body-muscles, without which so many strokes cannot have their due certainty and power. The mere fact that it is possible or usual to play Squash without skill or science is not proof that skill and science cannot enter into Squash. It is possible to play Golf or Billiards or any other skilful and scientific game without any skill or science whatsoever.

We admit that Squash is generally a "selfish" game, each player playing for himself alone and not for his side. But this is just what pleases the average American, at any rate: he likes to be independent, and to be responsible for his own success or failure. Moreover, the larger-sized Squash-Courts admit of the Four-Game.

Last of all, though Squash is seldom played in the open air, yet it easily might be, especially if a good sliding roof were used; and, even if the best ventilated and best lighted Court is inferior to the open air Court, still the former can be used in all weathers and seasons.

And in America Squash has a further merit besides the above, with respect to *time*. Not only can it be played during frost or snow or rain (at Marlborough College we used to play it in the rain without a roof): in quite a short time enough exercise can be had to last for the whole day. In fact, when I go into a Squash-Court to "knock-up" by myself, I find that just a quarter of an hour gives me all the exercise I need: the game is so quick. Squash would therefore be the ideal exercise for short intervals between hours of work— it is the *multum in parvo* of Athletics.

And this calls to mind another point: Squash can be played by artificial light, as it is at New York, Boston, Haverford, Tuxedo, and elsewhere. Such light has never yet been a great success for Tennis (Court-Tennis), Lawn-Tennis, or Racquets.

Passing from the idea of time to the idea of place and space, we must remember that Squash needs only a small surface: 20 feet by 40 is more than enough for the whole building (see Chapter I). Indeed, an unused room, or a stable, or a cellar, can easily be turned into a Squash-Court; or even a single wall of a house can be utilized. The game, therefore, need not entail much initial expense; and, besides this, there are plenty of Courts and there will be more and more every year in various parts of the country.

Regarded as exercise, Squash is not too severe, at any rate for the feet and legs; yet it will bring on a good sweat in half an hour, and will thus purify the blood, and improve the circulation (especially in the hands and feet) far more healthily than hot air or steam. It will remove superfluous fat, and bring quicker action of the stomach and bowels, and thus help to prevent indigestion and constipation, especially if (Chapters V and VIII) the body be moved in the right way. It will develope the lungs, and will fill them with oxygen, if the Court be ventilated properly. Besides this, if occasionally the Court be used for (Hand-) Fives (Chapter XII), the left arm and left side will receive a share of the work.

Some of the above advantages might be claimed for other forms of exercise, such as Bowling, Bicycling, Running, and Gymnastics. But these do not offer the same inducements as a game: they do not give the same quick changes to meet an opponent's tactics;

they have not the joy of competitive games, however well they may serve the Germans, and those who can get exercise in no other form.

This joy has a real effect on the nerves and on the blood: it acts like a powerful tonic; just as anger may act like a poison. The effect has been proved chemically: the blood is actually altered by joy.

And then there is the recreation and change, not mere muscular exertion, nor yet mere rest for the mind, but the turning of the mind into a new channel of activity—which after all, is often the very truest rest.

For in Squash the mind seems to have just the right amount of work to do: it should be alert and prompt and ready to make or change its plan in a moment; it should turn its plan into action; it should study and estimate the opponent and his strong and weak points, it should study the "self" and its strong and weak points, and should correct the latter between whiles; it should be original and free within the limits of the written laws of the game and the unwritten laws of honour.

So Squash, like many other games, should really help to form character: steady correction of faults one by one, self-control as opposed to careless negligence and impatience, these and many other qualities may be devel-

INTRODUCTION xix

oped, as well as that fairness in competition, of which we spoke just now.

Nor is this all. Squash should not merely be good for the development of the body, good for health, good for the mind, and good for the character, but it should also have a general social influence. If the right Handicaps were carefully arranged (see Chapter XII), players of the greatest and smallest skill could easily meet at Squash, and *inter-sex* Matches could be arranged.

Squash is a grand game for ladies, who need healthy exercise, if they are ever to be healthy mothers of healthy children. Ladies are, almost without exception, wonderfully keen on the game, and boys, elderly men, business-men, and clerks, and many others, find it just the very thing they need. It is even possible for the lover of solitude to have an inter-self competition!

The chief reason why the game will be so popular with these various classes is that it is not too difficult. Nearly any one can easily reach a fair standard of play, which may be called "the stage of enjoyment".

And this is only the beginning, since from Squash it is very easy to pass to other games, for instance Racquets, Tennis (Court-Tennis), and Lawn-Tennis. Personally, I should go so far as to assert that it may be a mistake for most people even to try these games, (or at any rate the first two), until they have mastered Squash, and learnt at Squash the positions and movements of the racket, the body, the arms, and the feet, and the angles at which the ball comes off from the floor and from the walls. If I had to learn Tennis (Court-Tennis) over again, I should certainly learn Squash first: even now I find that the very best practise for a fast game of Court-Tennis is a quarter of an hour in a Squash-Court with a Court-Tennis racket and a Lawn-Tennis ball.

So it seems that Squash need not be merely a children's game after all—if only it be properly taught and learnt. There lies that difficulty, which it is my ambition to lessen.

CHAPTER I.

THE COURT AND IMPLEMENTS DESCRIBED: WITH SUGGESTIONS.

IN the following pages I shall offer various suggestions, some of which will be found in detail under their proper headings: these will be printed in small type. The rest will be collected at the end of the Chapter.

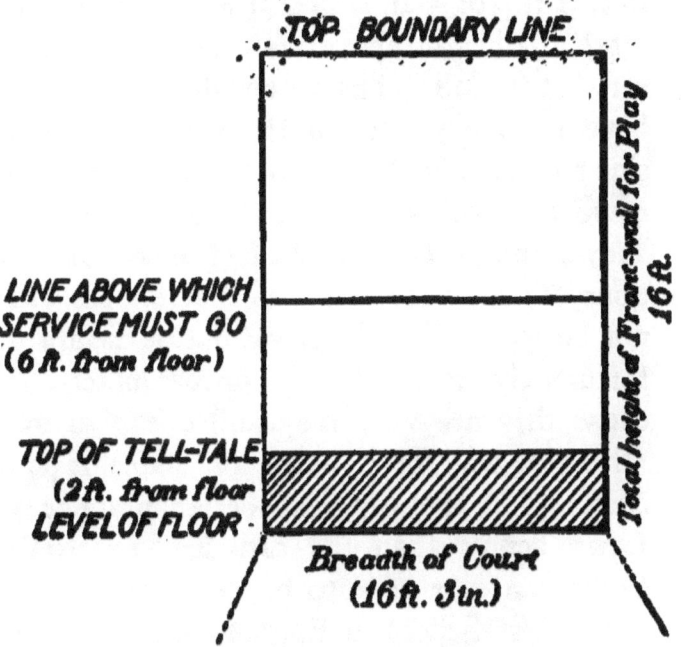

1. FRONT-WALL OF A SQUASH COURT.

I shall be very glad if any readers will offer criticisms or notes about their own experiences. These would be invaluable in case this little work should reach a second edition.

Part I. : The Court :

A Squash-Court may consist of only one wall, the Front-wall. On this wall, usually at the height of 2 ft. [2 ft. 6 in.] from the ground, is a broad strip of tin, or some other material, to mark the height above which the ball must hit the wall. Over this "tell-tale" is another line, 6 ft. [or 5 ft. 9 in.] from the ground, to mark the height above which the server must serve the ball. The one-walled Court will have boundary lines at the places where the side and back-walls of an ordinary Court would come (see below); it will also have nettings above, and on both sides of (i. e. as continuations of) the Front-wall, so that the balls may not be lost. The Single-wall Courts are unfortunately rare. I say unfortunately, because they are very easy and cheap to make (the side-wall of a house or stable is sufficient), and they are far better practice for Lawn-Tennis than the ordinary four-walled Court can ever hope to be.

My first School in England used to have a two-walled Court, the second wall being on the left of the Front-wall: some Courts have

COURT AND IMPLEMENTS 3

it on the right. The other side and the back are marked by boundary-lines. This also made a capital game.

At Marlborough College, we had many three-walled Courts, the two side-walls sloping down from the front-wall, and the back-wall being marked by a boundary-line, as before.

These Courts we also used for Hand-fives. Mr. F. H. Hewitt was one of the best players at these two games, which encouraged the player to place the ball down the sides of the Court.

But far the commonest type of Court is the four-walled Court, whether it has a roof or not. The four walls give the best preparation and practice for Tennis (Court-Tennis) and Racquets.

The measurements vary considerably: there is at present no single recognized standard. This has the advantage of variety in the games at different places, and it allows of almost any room or corner being converted into a Squash-Court. But, as there seems a very good prospect of many Squash competitions before long, it may be as well to give what seem the best measurements: they work very well at Tuxedo and elsewhere, and are likely to be accepted by the great majority of players, even if some experts prefer the larger-sized Court such as they have at Lord's Cricket Ground in England.* This latter Court is far better suited to the small ball and the light racket. In Amer-

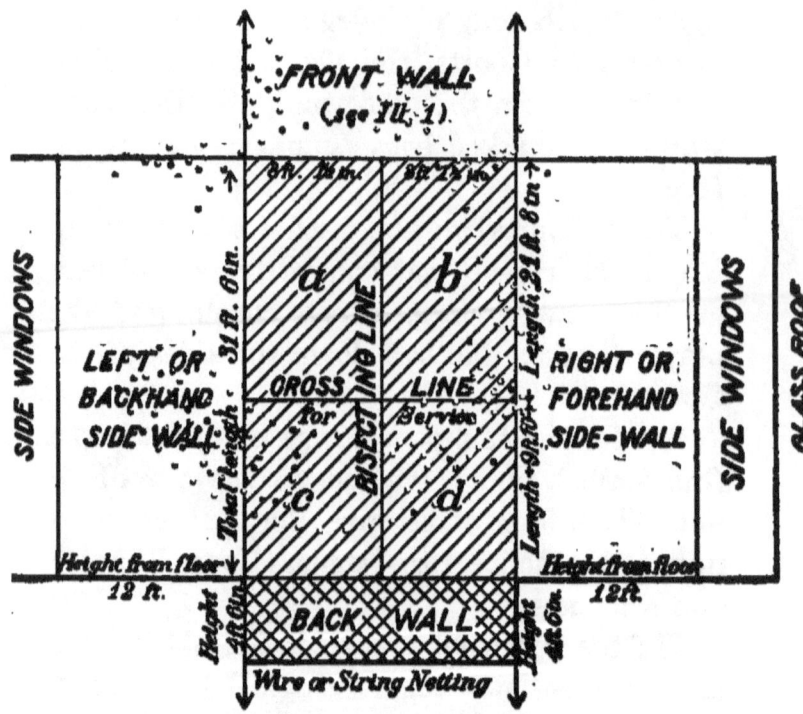

2. (a) PLAN OF A SQUASH COURT.

ica the Lawn Tennis ball and (small) Lawn Tennis racket are the usual implements.

                                                  ft.   in.
Length of Floor (see below)..31 6 [31.4]
Breadth .. ..16 3 [17.0]

* The Lord's Court is 42 ft. by 24 ft. 1 in.; the heights are:—of the Back-wall 8 ft. 8 in., of the Service-line 8 ft. 9 in., of the tell-tale 2 ft. 4 in. The Cross-Court line is 23 ft. 1-2 in. from the Front-wall.

COURT AND IMPLEMENTS

Height of   ft. in.
   Back-wall (see below) 4   6 [5.0]
   Side-walls (boundary-line) ..12 0 [12.6]
   Front-wall
      boundary-line 16
      service-line .. .. 6 0 [5.9]
      top of tell-tale—(but see be-
          low)— .. .. 2 0 [2.6]

2. (b.) MODEL OF A SQUASH COURT. (*To be cut out*).

Floor-lines,   ft. in.
   Service-line (from Side-wall to Side-wall) from the Front-wall 21   8

Dividing-line (from Front-wall to Back-wall), down the centre of the Court.

Double Courts should be a few feet longer but about half as broad again, say 34 ft. by 24 ft.

I have preferred to use this measurement not only because it gives an excellent game (especially with the movable tell-tale), but also because it gives *the measurements which are at present commonest in America;* whereas, in England, there is far greater variety. Thus at Cambridge we had one Racquet-Court (60 ft. by 30 ft.) divided into three Squash-Courts (30 ft. by less than 20 ft.), while the Squash-Court at Lord's is ever so much larger. At one Public School alone we played Squash in Courts of at least three different sizes.

   The Length of the Floor, as given here, is from the Front-wall to the Back-wall, and does not include the space for spectators behind the Back-wall. The larger this space is, the more spectators the *Dedans,* as they call it at Tennis (Court-Tennis), will be able to contain, and the better the Court will be ventilated. The floor of the *Dedans* should be raised several feet, so that the spectators may see well over the Back-wall; the rows behind the front row

COURT AND IMPLEMENTS 7

should be raised still more, like the seats of an amphitheatre.

It is much better to have the Back-wall low, even if a ball does sometimes go over it at its first bounce, than to have it high, with a boundary-line painted at 4 ft. 6 in. from the ground, and a gallery above. For in such a Court the spectators are too high up to see the play satisfactorily: this high Gallery is the great disadvantage of Racquet-Courts. We need hardly say that a high Back-wall without any boundary-line is an absurdity; it encourages players to hit hard and high, so as to bring the ball from the Back-wall right up to the front of the Court; this is a poor stroke. The low Back-wall will discourage this stroke, it will give the spectators a better and more comfortable view of the play, and it will keep the Court itself better ventilated. Squash players are indebted to Tom Pettitt for this excellent idea.

The back of the *Dedans* can have a wall made of windows (or storm-sashes) which could be either shaded or opened (or removed) in summer: this would make Squash as nearly as possible an out-of-door game.

The Court should be ventilated not only above but also below (e. g. below the tell-tale). In a cool and well-ventilated Court there may not be the same amount of sweating, but more exercise may be taken with more pleasure and with less fatigue. and the extra oxygen will purify the blood and improve its circulation. Those who have a tendency to Consumption should play Squash quietly in a well-ventilated Court.

A sliding glass roof would be the ideal roof. It used to work very well in a Fives-Court in England, though, if it is not carefully made and constantly attended to, it is almost bound to leak.

The Side-walls may have their boundary line even lower than 12 ft. 0 in. But of course there may be windows or a wall above this: side-windows as well as top-windows are good for ventilation and light. The higher the roof, the better the air. But the windows should be made so that they may be shaded or opened or shut at a moment's notice. The usual delay of ten minutes is most annoying. The top of the tell-tale (which in a wooden Court is usually made of tin, so that a ball which hits it may give a special sound) is at present of the same height as in a Racquet-Court; and this height is best for beginners and for those who play chiefly for exercise. But skilful players feel the need of a lower line, so that they may "kill" a weak return by their opponent. As it is, there is very little chance of killing any ball at all. In other words, the Squash-Court, if it is to be a miniature Racquet-Court, should have the tell-tale *in proportion,* i. e. lower than in a Racquet-Court. But how can both heights be given by the same tell-tale?

The tell-tale need not be fixed. In the corner-angles of the Front-wall there can be placed pegs at various heights, to fit into holes in the tell-tale. The higher position would, as I say, be better for ladies and for beginners.

The Dividing or Bisecting line, from front to back, will be found useful in Handicaps, especially where one player has to confine his strokes to one half of the Court (Chapter XI).

The Court admits of plenty of "varieties" which Mr. H. S. Mahony would call "furniture"; but I should advise that these should be movable. Thus a movable buttress, e. g. like the *Tambour* of a Ten-nis (Court-Tennis) Court, could be put on one Side-

COURT AND IMPLEMENTS

wall; this would be fine practice for the latter game; and a triangular pillar would serve the purpose excellently. Or, again, there can be openings (movable doors) in the Side- or Back-wall, as practice for the *Dedans* or *Grille* of Court-Tennis. Or advantage might be taken (as at Harrow School, the nursery of Squash) of natural unevenness in the walls, such as pipes, windows, etc. A great friend of mine, Mr. E. F. Benson, the author of " Dodo ", has a genius for devising such obstacles and hazards.

The whole of the top of the Court should be painted white, or white-washed. This makes all the difference in the light. The same applies to Racquet and Court-Tennis Courts.

As to the material of the Court, in America it is usually wood: a double thickness, with sawdust between it and the solid outside walls, is of course to be preferred. I imagine that the wood-bricks, such as they used to have at Queen's Club in the Covered Lawn-Tennis Courts, might be even better; or, probably, glazed bricks would be excellent. On the front wall the planks should present their *edges* to the players.

Personally I prefer a Cement-Court, if hard balls are to be used. Wood is cheap, but it is also rather noisy, so that the use of a hard ball, a Racquet or Fives of Tennis (Court-Tennis) ball is almost out of the question: this prevents wooden Squash from being really first-rate practice for Racquets or Court-Tennis. I remember that, at Marlborough,

Mr. Benson and myself used to get splendid practice for Racquets by using Racquet-balls in a cement Squash-Court. Cement is more satisfactory than stone slabs, and of course Bickley's cement, though expensive, is far the best.

The colour of a Cement-Court would naturally be chocolate or dark grey or grey or white: if white balls (e. g. Lawn-Tennis balls) are used, then the chocolate or dark grey may be best. Bickley's stain has been found excellent for darkening the shade and increasing the " fastness " of cement: it quite altered the Tennis (Court-Tennis) Court at Brighton.

But, if the Court be of wood, then the colour should probably be either red or green: on the top of the colour can be a coating of shellac. The red we have found to be satisfactory where the Courts are to be lighted artificially in the evening: it is said that a dark colour (dark green, for example,) will soak up too much of the light. The Courts in New York and Tuxedo are red.

I cannot believe that any colour can be better than green, at least for play at daylight. As to play by electric light or gas, this may be helped either by white upper-walls and roof, or by a sheet drawn across the Court above the light, which should be cast upwards onto the sheet. Only the sheet must not hinder the ventilation.

I have already spoken of top-lights and side-lights, and I have just been led to speak of evening lights. The problem is all-important for business-men and brain-workers in general.

At present a very fair light is given by large electric or gas lamps (preferably incandescent) with their glass somewhat opaque or frosted, and protected by metal trellis or crate-work. But I believe that the true solution of the problem lies in

(a) the above mentioned use of the white sheet either above or below the lights: this has been suggested to me by Messrs. Richmond Fearing and Lawrence Stockton, the well-known Tennis (Court-Tennis) players; or

(b) the use of glass *prisms*, by means of which it is possible to light even an underground cellar. This was suggested by a member of the New York Racquet and Tennis Club.

For the benefit of those—and there will be many more of them every year—who would like to build Squash-Courts either for their own private use, or for a regular Club, or for a more or less informal Club of those who want exercise, Mr. James B. Lord, the Architect, has most kindly made for me and allowed me to use the design which is given at the end of the book. He has also obtained estimates for me, and these will, I hope, do much to make this little book really practical.

The expense of building a single Court will depend a great deal on the following conditions:—

(i) the number of walls required for the Court (see above);

(ii) the number of walls already available (e. g. the corner walls of the house and stable might give two);

(iii) the height of the Court above the top boundary-lines;

(iv) the amount of lighting, whether by roof alone, or by side windows alone (this is seldom satisfactory, at least without prisms), or by both;

(v) the nature and quality of the "outside" materials (stone or brick or plaster or wood, etc.);

(vi) the nature and quality of the "inside" materials for floor and walls (Bickley cement, cheaper cement, double wood, single wood);

(vii) the nature and level of the substratum.

Assuming, however, that one four-walled Court is required, that there is no wall already existing, that both top-lights and side-lights are required, that the out-side as well as the inside will be of wood, the inside being double and of stained and shellaced wood, then the cost of a Court should certainly not exceed 1500 dollars, provided that the foundations are already sound and the ground fairly level. See the end of the book.

To the above suggestions (in small type) let me now add one or two of a general kind before passing on to the implements of the game.

Close to the Court there should be a bath or shower, with hot water as well as cold: It is usually safer to begin with hot and to finish up with cold. The best form of heat, however, is the Steam- or Hot-air Cabinet, which is not only cheaper but also healthier than the

COURT AND IMPLEMENTS 13

ordinary Turkish Bath, since it leaves the head cool and allows the pure air to be inhaled.

This Cabinet will continue the sweat which the Squash has already started. After the cool or cold bath or shower or sponging, a little gentle exercise should be taken: the Ballgame Apparatus will be found to give the just right kind and amount.

Every large Club, every University, and every School, should certainly have Squash-Courts for its members. Mere Gymnasia will never achieve anything like the same results.

And private houses should have their Squash-Courts too. In the country, where land is cheap, this is easy enough; but how about town? Here any little-used room can be turned into a Squash-Court permanently or for the time being. I have played Squash with Mr. Benson in many of the rooms at Lambeth Palace; and once we even played out on the roof.

This suggests the use of flat roofs for Squash-Courts: the conditions are good, so far as concerns space and light and air, three all-important requisites. One wall or more, an even floor, and plenty of twine or string netting, and, if possible, some sort of a roof (see above), and all that need be added. Mr. Robert Bacon thought of having a Court on his house in New York.

Or else an outside-wall of the house can be used. In this case one might have to level the floor, and perhaps build one or two Side-walls. But the expense would be slight.

Anyhow it is essential that every member of the household (if ours were a true Democracy we would include the well-fed servants) should have an opportunity for daily exercise, and not only an opportunity for it but an inducement to it. If ladies would only play Squash instead of driving and going to concerts and theatres and at-homes, and paying calls or playing cards, if they would only get some of their social life in this way, they and their children would be happier and healthier than they are, and, in case the fact should influence them, I will not say less ugly, gauche, and fat, for of course they are never this, but, if possible, more beautiful, graceful, and neat in figure.

Let me mention here, especially for the benefit of those who live in the country, or like to entertain their friends, that it is not much, not so very much harder or dearer, to build two or three Courts than to build one, especially if the Front-wall of the Court is already there, being, for instance, the side-wall of the house or stable. The two Side-walls of the first Court will serve as the Side-walls of the second and third Courts, which will only need

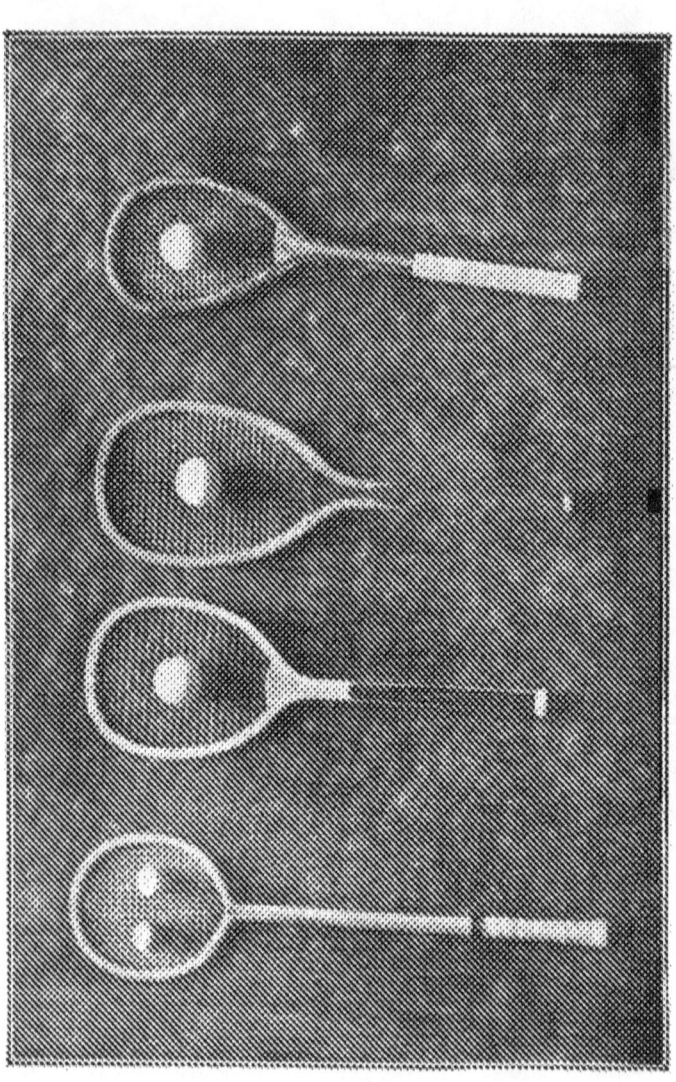

3. VARIOUS RACKETS AND BALLS FOR SQUASH.

Beginning at the left, we have (a) Racquet bat and two Squash-Racquet balls; the Squash-Racquet bat is a little shorter, and the Racquet ball a little smaller; (b) Squash-Tennis bat (America) and Lawn Tennis ball; (c) Lawn Tennis bat and ditto; (d) Tennis (Court-Tennis)

the Back-walls, the outer Side-walls, the roof and windows, and the wood or cement for the Court itself. For a Club or School or University the advantages of several Courts over one Court are that they do not cost more to keep up, that they bring in considerably more money, and that they encourage more people to come, on the chance of getting a game.

For other suggestions which apply rather to the game itself (for example the occasional use of Lawn-Tennis scoring at Squash), I must refer to Chapters XI and XII.

Since I wrote the above, Mr. W. H. Patten suggested to me that various men, especially those who were busy in the day-time, might easily subscribe and build a rough-and-ready Court on a vacant lot of ground. The expense for each man would be far smaller than that of a private Court, and the wives and families and friends of the men could play in the morning. A movable Court, like a movable cottage, is a possibility deserving of consideration.

Part II. The Implements.

The Illustration will give an idea of the relative sizes and shapes of some of the rackets and balls which can be used at Squash. It will be seen that, quite apart from the different ways of Scoring (Chapter II), and the different Handicaps (Chapter XI), the game admits of different forms of great variety.

This variety should be utilised not only for the sake of a pleasant change, but also as a preparation for various *Games:* the Tennis (Court-Tennis) racket, with a Tennis or Lawn-Tennis ball, can be chosen as a preparation for Tennis, the Lawn-Tennis or Squash-Racquet bat, with a small india-rubber or a Racquet ball, for Racquets, and so on.

In England the commonest implements are the small india-rubber ball and the small Racquet bat; in America they are the Lawn-Tennis ball and the small Lawn-Tennis (or Squash-Tennis) bat. Let us begin with the latter.

Americans generally use a Lawn-Tennis ball (Slazenger's or Wright and Ditson's seem to be the best at present), and a Squash-Tennis racket, which is like a miniature Lawn-Tennis racket: this can be bought for a few dollars from these firms.

Those who play or who intend to play Tennis (Court-Tennis) are advised to use the Tennis racket when they play Squash, and to use the Tennis stroke also, regardless of the fact that it is not the best stroke for a winning game. But I can promise them that they will get more and better practice for the positions of the body and racket, for the ordinary returns,

COURT AND IMPLEMENTS 17

for volleys and half-volleys, and for strokes off the Back- and Side-walls, in a quarter of an hour's play in the Squash-Court than in several hours' play in the Tennis Court itself. The reason is that the ball comes back to them almost immediately, owing to the closeness of the Front- and Side-walls.

Lawn-Tennis players should of course use the Lawn-Tennis racket, whatever Lawn-Tennis stroke they may decide to adopt: see further Chapter XII. Slazenger's "Doherty" or E. G. M. racket is among the best, and Wright and Ditson's "Pym" is also very popular.

Suppose, however, that the players use the small india-rubber balls, as they do in England, then they may get their balls from Prosser in Pentonville Road, London, or from Moore, the Racquet Professional at the Tuxedo Tennis and Racket Club, Tuxedo Park, New York. The balls may be white or black or red, according to the colour of the Court; and they may be large or small, the smaller being about the size of a Racquet ball, the larger about the size of a Fives (Hand-Fives) ball.

The racket may be either a Lawn-Tennis or Squash-Tennis racket (see above), or a Racquet bat, or, preferably, a small-sized Racquet bat, which is called a Squash-Racquet bat. Slazenger and Prosser provide these.

If the Court be a Cement Court, as I should

certainly recommend, then to these balls may be added:—

(a) The Court-Tennis ball, to be used with a Court-Tennis racket.

(b) The Racquet ball, to be used with a Racquet or Squash-Racquet bat: these balls can be had from Prosser's, in the Pentonville Road, London.

(c) A miniature Racquet-ball, to be used with the same Racket as (b).

Additional implements of the Cement-Court would be:—

(d) The wooden bat, in the shape of a narrow hand-mirror; Slazenger has it in his Bat-Fives sets. The ball would be as in (b) or (c) or (e); this Game is called Bat-Fives in England.

(e) The hands with or without gloves; the ball would be an enlarged Racquet ball; this game is called Fives or Hand-Fives, the "Fives" being at first an expression for the five fingers.

In the small Court with a Back-wall there is some danger in the use of these hard little balls, especially by beginners. I have never yet seen any harm done, but then I may have been exceptionally fortunate.

(f) In Chapter XII. I shall explain the value of Handicap-implements, e. g. a narrow bat or piece of wood, or a cricket bat: among

COURT AND IMPLEMENTS 19

other merits, they compel the stronger player not only to play up his very hardest but also to be careful and accurate as to his position and timing of the stroke. They point out his weaknesses and faults better than any other means, since the smallest inaccuracy is exaggerated and proves fatal.

(g) When you break a racket, don't throw it away, but keep the handle for practice outside the Court: the use and advantage will be explained in Chapter VIII.

And now as to the choice of a Squash-Racket.

The weight is of less importance than the balance, which should be about the place where the screw comes (though this is not always a good test). Be careful that the wood has no flaw: flaws are often concealed by an artful coating of paint or varnish! Beware also of inferior gut: there is a splendid opening for any one who will provide the Racket-maker with consistently good and reliable gut. At present no such maker has appeared upon the scene; the guts of Messrs. Turner, of Quinn Street, Chicago, and Messrs. Tracy, of Cowgate Street, London, are the best that I know of. There is a fortune waiting for some one here.

The handle should not be too thin: a thick handle soon becomes pleasant to the grip. In

England the best Lawn-Tennis players have enormous handles to their rackets. Slazenger sometimes covers the handles, and this is an excellent plan.

Be sure to keep the racket in a Press. Presses cost little to start with, and they save expense in rackets and gut every year. A warped frame seldom recovers itself completely.

About clothing I need say very little.

Flannels I have always found to be more satisfactory than cotton or other materials: there seems to be less risk of catching cold afterwards. Round the waist there should be, if anything, a good broad belt.

Many players find that the feet feel less tired if two pairs of socks are worn instead of one. I believe that a large number of New York and Boston players wear two pairs. The shoes should of course have soles of india-rubber (or soft felt); if the india-rubber is not soft, or even if it is soft, a number of holes in the sole may help to give the feet a better grip of the ground. Good shoes are sold by "Newman the Shoeman", at Boston, Mass. They are expensive, but in the end are very cheap, because they last so long. Slazenger sells good shoes at a cheaper price.

CHAPTER II.

THE GAME AND ITS RULES.

The underlying principle of the Single game at Squash is that two players try alternately to hit the ball up against the Front-wall, above the tell-tale on the Front-wall; the players must hit the ball before the second bounce. The player who first fails to hit the ball above the tell-tale before the second bounce loses the point.

So far the idea is simple, and very like the idea of Lawn-Tennis. except that in Lawn-Tennis you have

(a) a net to hit over, instead of a tell-tale to hit above;

(b) an opponent facing you, instead of facing in the same direction as you are.

(c) In Lawn-Tennis you also have limit lines outside of which the ball must not bounce. Here the ordinary game of four-walled Squash differs: a ball which bounces full onto the Side-wall or Back-wall below a certain height is not "out" but in-play: it comes back into the Court.

Here lies one of the main claims of the

game—this play off the Side-walls and the Back-wall, which gives you a chance to get up a ball which has passed you. Lawn-Tennis needs greater accuracy and greater restraint, for it seldom allows of this second chance. And it is chiefly for this reason that Lawn-Tennis may be a better game than Squash, but is never likely to be so popular unless certain radical changes are introduced.

(*A Miss.*)

We spoke of two players hitting the ball alternately, until one of them *misses it*, either by actually missing it altogether, or by hitting it after its second bounce, or by sending it below the tell-tale, or, let us now add, by sending it above the upper boundary-line, or full onto any part of himself or his racket.* The player who first hits the ball, and thus starts it going, is called the Server.

It is usual to " toss up " (a coin or a racket) to decide which of the two players shall serve.

We said just now that the player who first misses a stroke, in the rally or round, loses the rally. The different ways of scoring will count this winning and losing of the rally differently.

---

* Some rules count the point against the striker if the ball hits him while it is still in play, i. e. before it has bounced twice. This is a good rule and is the rule in Racquets.

THE GAME AND ITS RULES 23

1. *The First Method, or Racquet-Scoring.*
The commonest method is as follows:

(*Service.*)
A serves the ball directly onto the Front-wall above the higher or Service-line: he has to stand with one foot behind the cross-court line, until he has served.

If A serves the ball on a Side-wall first, or below the higher or Service-line, or with both feet in front of the cross-court line, or into the wrong court (see below), then he is said to have served a *Fault:* two Faults in succession lose A the rally.

According to some rules, B is allowed, as in Racquets, and in order to save delay, to take the first Fault, if he likes. But, if he once tries to take it, the Service is no longer reckoned as a Fault.

According to one set of rules, he must make the ball pitch within the space marked *a* or *b* (between the Front-wall and the cross-court line) : see the Ground-plan above. According to another set of rules, he must make the ball pitch within the space marked *c* or *d* (between the Back-wall and the cross-court line).

In his first Service he can take his choice between serving from the *a b* side (left side) into the *c d* side (right side), or *vice versa;* his second service must be from the opposite side.

He must always serve across the Court, and never down his own side.

B has to take the service, and according to some rules he may volley it, as in Racquets. According to other rules, he must let it pitch on the ground first. This is not so good.

Supposing A, the Server, wins the rally, and B loses it, then A scores an "ace", the actual Score being A "1-0" or A "1-love". Supposing A, the Server, wins the next rally, and B loses it, then A scores another "ace" (A "2-0" or "2-love"); and so on.

But supposing A, the Server, loses the rally, and B wins it, then no "ace" is scored, but B goes in to serve instead of A.

If B, the server, now wins the next rally, he scores an "ace" ("1-x"), and, if he wins the next rally, he scores an "ace" ("2-x"); if he loses it, then no "ace" is scored, and A goes in to serve again.

In other words, only the server can score "aces": the non-server has to win a rally before he can serve, and then another rally before he can score an "ace".

The game is won by the player who first reaches 15 "aces".

(*Setting.*)

If the Score is "13-all", then the player who has lost the last rally decides whether the

THE GAME AND ITS RULES

game shall be played straight out (e. g. "14-13" or "game-ball 13", then "15-13" or "game"), or whether he and his opponent shall "*set*". If he chooses the latter, then the rest of the game depends on a new little game for 3 or 5 aces, whichever he may prefer.

Similarly, if the score is "14-all" or "game-ball all", then he may choose whether the game shall be played straight out, the single ace deciding it, or whether he and his opponent shall "set"; in which case the new little game will be for 3 aces.

2. *Second, or Reversed-Racquets Method.*

After losing the toss, A serves as before (see 1.)

Supposing A, the Server, wins the rally, he does not score an "ace" (as in 1); but B now goes in to serve.

Supposing B, the Server, loses the rally, and A wins it, A now at last scores the "ace" ("1-0" or "1-love"); if B, the server, loses the next rally also, A scores another ace, ("2-0" or "2-love"); and so on, B serving until he can win a rally.

The game is for 15, as before, and the Setting also is as before.

According to this second method, then, the server can not score an "ace": the server has to win a rally and to become the non-server before he can score an "ace".

3. *Third, or Every-Point Method.*

A variation of the First or of the Second Method is that every rally gives an "ace" to the winner of it. The Service may be decided according to the First or Second Methods, or the players may serve alternately, each having one or else two services at a time. The latter is the better way.

This game may be found useful in certain Handicap-Matches (see Chapter XI). It is recommended as an occasional change in the Scoring of Racquets also, and it shares with the Fourth or Lawn-Tennis Method the advantage that every point counts as a full "ace".

4. *Fourth, or Lawn-Tennis Method.*

The scoring here is exactly like the scoring in Lawn-Tennis, with which the reader is probably already familiar.

The Match may be for the best of 3 or 5 sets. A set is won by 6 games, though, at "5 games all", deuce and vantage Sets may be played, if this is the regular custom of the Court or is agreed upon between the players.

The players serve in alternate games, throughout.

THE GAME AND ITS RULES 27

A serves as before. If he wins, the score is "15-love",—if he loses, it is "love-fifteen". If the score reaches "40-all" or "deuce", then we have vantage, deuce, vantage, game", or the older plan of "deuce, vantage, vantage-all, game" may be preferred, as being less tedious.

This Method, like the Second and Third, prevents a player from scoring a large number of "aces" in succession simply by service. Good service is an advantage, but not too overwhelming an advantage.

(*Lets.*)

In Lawn-Tennis and Tennis (Court-Tennis), the opponents are on opposite sides of the net and do not interfere with one another: so, except on out-of-the-way occasions, neither can claim a "let" or hindrance except when one player gives the ball before his opponent is ready; of course a good deal must be left to A's feelings of honour.

Now in this case A can claim a "*let*", provided that he has not tried to take the ball.* This rule is constantly ignored, and a player will have a try at a ball: if he makes a good stroke, then he seldom dreams of claiming a

---

* The same applies to a ball which hits the netting above the low Back-wall after its first bounce, otherwise this netting is 'out of Courts.'

let; if not, then he claims a "let", i. e. he claims to play the rally over again.

This rule, viz. that A cannot claim a "let" if he has tried at the ball, holds good whether A was not ready or whether B was in his way, unless B was so much in his way that the stroke was impossible (e. g. if A's racket actually hit B).

A can also claim a "let" if he has hit a ball which would have gone above the tell-tale had it not hit B: a rough-and-ready rule is that the ball must be a rising ball and must hit B above the knee. But this is not quite satisfactory, and the best question to ask is " Would the ball have gone up if it had not hit B?"

So far we have considered unreadiness and actual obstruction; but what if B obstructed the sight of A, whether by accident or on purpose? Some say that, so long as B does not move, he has a right to obstruct A's sight, and I have noticed that not a few players purposely bar the way at Racquets as well as Squash: I call to mind some players who bob about in front of the opponent, and yet keep just so far away from the ball that the opponent does not like to leave the ball alone and claim a "let". We hope that this unsporting desire, to win at all costs, will soon disappear. It is not an integral part of the best game: there is plenty of chance of winning by other means.

THE GAME AND ITS RULES 29

The Implements will now be described, and the Handicaps will follow in a separate Chapter; but, even without them, it must be clear that it would be far more correct to describe Squash as many games in one than as a single monotonous game that requires no skill or adaptability.

CHAPTER III.

DIFFICULTIES AND FAULTS OF PLAYERS.

IN this Chapter I wish to point out to the reader what his difficulties and faults are likely to be or to have been. I hope that every time he comes to any place where he says " Yes, I quite agree ", that is, every time these suppositions seem to hit the mark, he will be encouraged to put in practice the suggestions which will be given in the subsequent Chapters.

The ideal player has his grip, his positions, and his strokes not only correct, but so automatic that they require little or no thought or attention; he makes certain of his easy strokes; his Backhand is at least as good as his Forehand; he can vary the place and pace and cut etc. of his strokes, and can conceal and mask these differences; he is alert, quick, and prompt; he anticipates his opponent's strokes; he is in good training and has a good " eye ", and he is always calm and patient and good-tempered.

But all this is very abstract and unpractical

DIFFICULTIES AND FAULTS

and, though it may help the reader to see several reasons why he has failed, it will be better to come down to the faults.

Have you ever realised all that is needed in order that one simple stroke may be a real and certain success? I grant that the stroke looks simple, and looks as if it were an indivisible unity; but have you ever realised how many things you may possibly be doing wrongly?

Take that first virtue, correctness: what things may be incorrect? The incorrect grip of the racket might account for much; thus you may be cramping yourself by having the thumb along the handle instead of across it.

You may be holding your racket with its head down before you make the stroke: if you are doing this, the stroke is likely to be a jerk or wrist-flick rather than a swing. You may also be holding your wrist wrong, your feet may be in the wrong position, facing forwards instead of facing the Side-wall.

Even if they are in the right position with respect to the Side-wall, they may yet be too far from the ball or too near it, too much in front of it or too much behind it. Or else you may still be on the move while you make the stroke, instead of being already in position.

This again may be due to a want of readiness, and is an especially common fault with those who wait " stugged " on their heels instead of alert on their toes. For ladies this latter position is extremely hard.

Or you may be in the right position, so far as your feet are concerned, and yet fail to use your left shoulder properly: you may have it too far forward before you begin the Backhand stroke, and too far back before you begin the Forehand stroke. Thus you will be losing much of the body-swing.

Or you may hit the ball when it is too high, or may fail to carry through the stroke, or you may slice the ball instead of meeting it with the full face of the racket, or you may not be keeping your eye on the ball.

So much for incorrectness. You will see that, if you attend to these points one by one, there is the chance of an almost unlimited improvement and progress. While the causes of error are so numerous, there is no reason to despair. There is no reason to assume that you never *will* improve. Do not assume it until you have practised the Exercises in Chapters VII, VIII, and IX, and have found them a failure.

But, even if you are doing all these things correctly, you may yet fail because you have to think about the corrections, instead of thinking about tactics, etc. There is only one way to get over this consciousness, viz. to pra tise and practise until these things, which should be the

4. WRONG POSITION.

DIFFICULTIES AND FAULTS 33

"indispensable mechanism" of the stroke, have become habitual, familiar, and sub-conscious, as the Psychologists would say.

Then and not till then will you be able to overcome the fault of missing many easy strokes, instead of making certain of them; and to overcome the weakness of the Backhander.

Then also your play will no longer be monotonous. Having the *mechanism* under your control, you will at length be able to direct it now in this direction, now in that, now with a cut, now without one; now slowly, and now fast.

No longer will your stroke be always slow, laborious, and stiff. These will be faults that, if you practise correctly, will wear off of themselves: the Piano-player soon forgets how stiff were her fingers during those Five-finger-Exercises. So far we have considered in what respects you may have failed rather than why you may have failed. Let us now consider this question.

You may have acquired bad habits of play (e. g. wrong grip, racket face held down, heels on ground, feet facing forwards instead of facing the Side-walls).

This may be because you have never been taught, or because you have been taught by a "natural" or genius-player, who himself did the whole stroke right by instinct, without knowing how or why.

Perhaps he told you of some fault, but did not tell you to correct it *per se*. He expected you to correct it during the game, when your attention was being distracted by ever so many other things; he expected you to correct the whole stroke at once, instead of concentrating your attention and your practice on just the incorrect part of it, and that too under the easiest possible conditions, e. g. in your own room.

Or perhaps you have been tired or in bad health and bad training, and so disinclined to keep on the alert and to attend to position: you merely wanted a game and a sweat.

Or during the game you have been impatient, possibly impatient to win; you have tried to make a killing stroke at once, and thus have risked too much in a game which is pre-eminently a game of safety. You ought to have been content to wait and lead up to an opening. Instead of this, you have begun at the top of your speed; you have volleyed as if you would smash the Front-wall to pieces, whereas you ought to have just met the ball.

Or, again owing to impatience, you may have tried to play Matches before you had played friendly games, to play friendly games before you had practised in the Court, and to practise

DIFFICULTIES AND FAULTS 35

in the Court before you had mastered the elementary positions and movements.

All these causes of failure seem to me to admit of being remedied, up to a certain point. But some of your failure may be due to physical defects, particularly to bad sight or a bad "eye". Diet may be of some use here; but at any rate do not conclude that these are certainly the reasons, or the chief reasons, why you or others fail, until you have found out by experience that the course of practice which I shall suggest can effect no sort of improvement.

CHAPTER IV.

THE HOLDING OF THE RACKET.

UNTIL a few years ago I used—among my other faults—to hold my racket quite wrongly. It was Smale, the well-known Racquet-coach at Wellington College, who first showed me this and some of my other faults. If I had thought out the matter, I should have realised that, with my former grip, I could scarcely expect to get a good swinging stroke which would hit the ball with the full face of the racket, fair and square. I had always held my racket wrongly by nature, which here was not at all a safe guide.

As soon as the new grip had grown easy and comfortable for me, then my stroke began to acquire more safety and more pace. But at first I found the change very unsatisfactory. I mention this so that others may be encouraged to persevere beyond the first few days or even weeks.

Although there may be exceptions, still the beginner should try at first to play with a swinging racket which shall offer its full face fair and square to the approaching ball. Be-

5. (I) BACKHAND: FINGERS OPEN.

5. (ii) BACKHAND: FINGERS CLOSED.

HOLDING OF THE RACKET

sides the swinging and full face, there is a third requisite: the racket should move for as long as possible in the line of the approaching ball, so that, in case one be a little too early or too late, the racket may still be meeting the ball in a line which shall carry the ball to the Front-wall. Fourthly, the racket should usually be gripped firmly during the stroke.

After the holding of the racket and the ordinary strokes have become familiar, then and not until then need one trouble about varying the grip and the pace.

I shall begin here with the *Backhand grip*, since most players are agreed as to what it should be.

Open your hand, as in Illustration 5 (i), and put the racket-handle so that the flat of it rests on the middle section of the First or Pointing Finger.

Now close the fingers over the handle, as in Illustration 5 (ii), keeping the fingers spread out rather than huddled together. Let the thumb go across the handle and not towards the face of the racket. This may have to be altered when you take a high ball backhanded, but you need not trouble about that at present.

Do not grip the handle too tightly before the racket begins to meet the ball: release the grip both before and after the stroke, and tighten it during the stroke.

Now bend the hand forward at the wrist, i. e. bend it towards the palm and the inside of the arm. Then during the stroke you can add extra pace by means of the wrist-movement.

What part of the handle should one hold? Should one hold the handle near to the end or nearer to the face? For ordinary purposes the hand might reach to about 3 inches from the end. But, if you have a weak wrist, or if you are taking a ball from close to the Back-wall, it might be better to hold the handle at a point far nearer to the face; this "clubbing" of the racket will give more certainty. For a hard drive, on the other hand, it may be better to hold the racket almost at the end.

Is this all? Is it enough to get the position of the fingers right, the tightness of the grip right, and the place on the handle right? No: there is one more point which is perhaps the most important of all, and this is to *keep the head of the racket up both before and after every stroke.*

What is the advantage of holding the racket like a hand-mirror? Well, it serves to protect the head; and it is the starting-point for the downward swing. If you held the racket with its face on the ground, you would have to give a jerk in order to strike the ball. The downward swing is almost as useful in Squash as it is in Golf. (See p. 39)

HOLDING OF THE RACKET 39

The actual position is not quite that of the hand-mirror: for the Backhand stroke the racket will be rather more to the left, for the Fore-hand stroke it will be rather more to the right.

A great deal of this will apply to the Forehand stroke. Here also the Hand-mirror position before and after the strokes is all-important; here also the grip should often be about 3 inches from the end of the racket, and not very tight except during the stroke itself; here

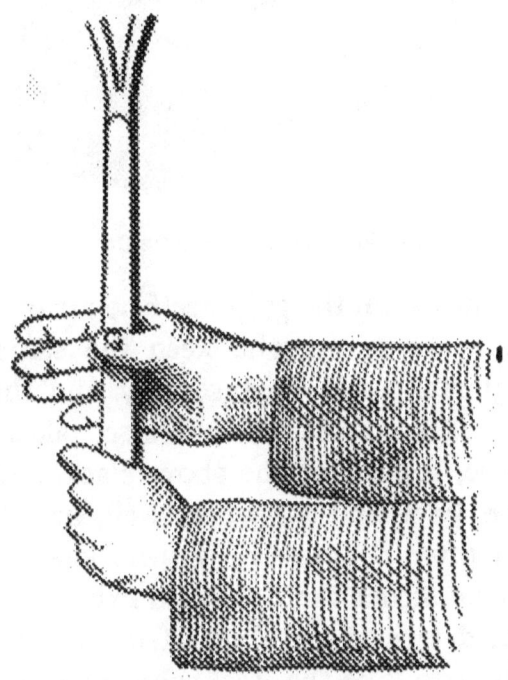

5. (iii) FOREHAND—FINGERS OPEN.

also the fingers should be spread out and not huddled too closely together. Here, however, the hand should be bent backwards at the wrist away from the palm.

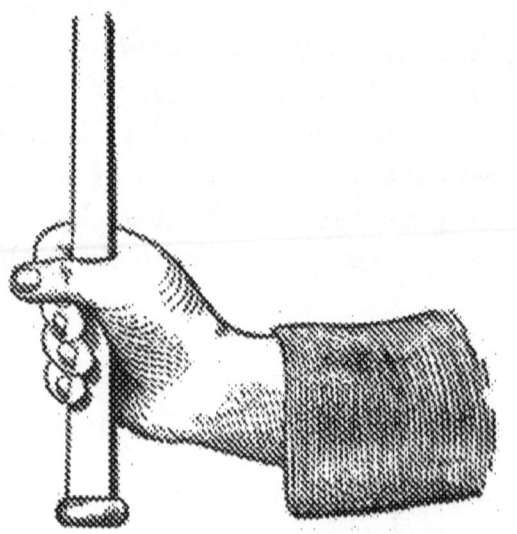

5. (iv) FOREHAND—FINGERS CLOSED.

But how shall the grip itself be arranged?

There are many who keep the same grip throughout, partly because they find that the change is inconvenient and also takes time. Of these, some keep the above Backhand grip for the Forehand stroke as well, and this is what I often do myself. Others keep for the Backhand stroke the Forehand grip which will now be described and illustrated.

This grip, like the Backhand grip, may not be comfortable at first, though there are many

HOLDING OF THE RACKET

who use it instinctively the very first time they handle a racket. Anyhow, as I know by experience, it may very soon be made familiar and easy by practice.

The best practice, as we shall see in Chapter VIII, is the use of the Racket-handle cut short. If we grant that each grip is really well adapted to its purpose, then the change of grip will be worth while, if only we can make it quickly enough. We can soon do this if we "drill" our muscles as we would drill them in practising the piano or violin. We can use the handle at all sorts of odd moments when otherwise our right hand would be idle.

What we want to do, anyhow, is to get one good grip or both good grips absolutely automatic and instinctive and unconscious before

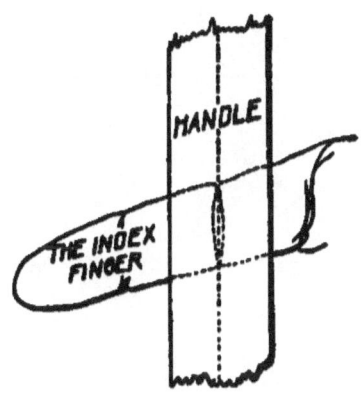

5. (v) Average Grip for both Backhand and Forehand Strokes.

we play our actual game or even before we go into the Court to practise or to have a lesson. For the right grip of the racket is one of the foundations of good playing.

An average grip is suggested for those who do not care to change.

CHAPTER V.

FOREHAND POSITION AND STROKE.

ASSUMING that the Forehand grip has now been mastered and has become an "inalienable possession" of the player, we shall next proceed to the Forehand position and stroke. The Ball-game Apparatus is recommended for him who wishes to make the position and stroke as much parts of his very self as the Forehand grip has now become the player's own. By means of this Apparatus the stroke can be repeated hundreds of times in a few minutes, and this too with little chance of a mistake, especially if the exercise be done before a looking-glass.

The player holds his racket, not too tightly, in the Hand-mirror position. Now what he wants to do is to meet the ball, which is approaching his right-hand side, full in the face with a swinging racket—a racket swinging towards the Front-wall.

If the player will think of himself as a clock and his arm and racket as the *pendulum* of that clock, he will get a good idea of the position which his body and feet should have. If the pendulum is to swing towards a Front-wall, it must face sideways. Then and only then will the arm and racket swing freely towards the Front-wall when the body and feet face the Side-wall: they should not face forwards, any more than they should at Golf or at Cricket.

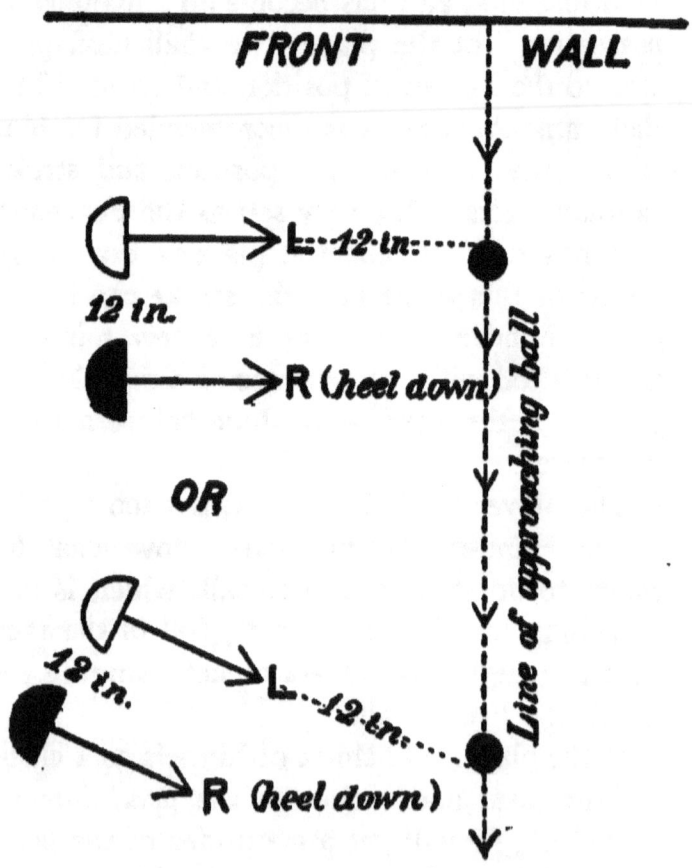

6. POSITION OF THE FEET FOR A FOREHAND STROKE.

FOREHAND POSITION

The Illustration will show how the feet should be placed for a Forehand Stroke, i. e. when the ball is coming to your right hand side as you look towards the Front-wall. The feet should be already in their position before the stroke begins: they should be about 12 inches apart, with the weight of the body resting chiefly on the back foot (the right foot). During the stroke the weight will pass forwards and onto the front foot (the left foot).

If the feet thus face the right Side-wall, the body will naturally face the right Side-wall also, since the feet are as it were the foundation of the body. Thus the pendulum, i. e. the arm and racket, will swing freely towards the Front-wall and towards the ball on the right, if the stroke starts with the racket lifted up and drawn back, somewhat as in Golf.

The feet are at times nearer to one another, at times further apart; at times they are taken unawares and are facing forwards. In this case the body at any rate should be facing sideways, turning on its hips as on a pivot.

If this turning on the hips be found a difficult process, then it should be practised (see Chapter VIII) as a special exercise.

But, if you can get the feet to face sideways, as in the Illustration, or even to face a little away from the Front-wall, the stroke will be ever so much better and safer.

The face, however, must be turned towards the approaching ball, even while the body is turned well to the right. Is this also a difficult process? Then the turning of the head from side to side (see Chapter VIII) should also be practised as a special exercise. This neck-exercise can easily be done during work, or during a walk: it will compel us to notice the scenery and surroundings! How too busy in mind we often are!

The same occasions will give us practice in holding the head up, or rather in holding the chin back. If the stroke starts with the head bent far forward, it will lose much of its force.

The player is now gripping his racket rightly and holding it in the Hand-mirror position and with the hand bent backwards from the palm; his feet face the right Side-wall; his face faces the approaching ball, and his chin is well back. Now let him bring his *left shoulder forwards,* not hesitating to hold the left hand up, if that will help him. Finally, let him move his racket up and back to the right from the Hand-mirror position, and he will be in the pose of Illustration 7: he will be ready to make a Forehand Stroke.

And now, having the Forehand position, he can make the Forehand stroke. Let him either imagine a ball to be let us say 12 inches in front of his left foot and 12 inches from

7. POSITION BEFORE A FOREHAND STROKE, EXAGGERATED.

FOREHAND POSITION

the ground, or let him arrange a ball thus on the Ball-game Apparatus. This imaginary or real ball he must strike right away from him, i. e. not across towards the left but out and away toward the right, so as to get freedom and to open out.

The racket will swing down and strike the ball; meanwhile the whole body will move forwards and round to the left, pivoting on the hips, and the body will pass its weight from the back foot (right) onto the front foot (left). The wrist, at first bent backwards, will also unbend itself as it meets the ball, and thus add an extra impetus.

These points may be summed up here, for the sake of convenience.

Throughout:—

(i) The feet face the right Side-wall; the eye is kept on the ball.

Before the stroke:—

(ii) the grip is correct;
(iii) the racket is up and back to the right;
(iv) the wrist is bent backwards away from the palm;
(v) the left shoulder is forward (the left hand may be held up);
(vi) the weight of the body is on the back (right) foot.

During the stroke:—

(vii) the grip is tightened;

(viii) the racket swings down and meets the ball, to which it is all the time exposing its full face; the racket should swing away and out freely towards the right;

(xi) the wrist straightens itself (it may even bend towards the palm) as the ball is being struck;

(x) the body swings round forward towards the left, on the hips as on a pivot;

(xi) the weight of the body passes from the back foot (right) onto the front foot (left).

After the stroke, notice the following points:—

(xii) the racket is carried through after the actual stroke (though not to the same extent as in Golf);

(xiii) it then returns to the Hand-mirror position;

(xiv) the wrist is now bent backwards again, away from the palm;

(xv) the body faces forwards;

(xvi) the weight of the body is evenly distributed between the two feet;

(xvii) the two feet face forwards (in the position which we shall give in Chapter VII);

(xviii) they rest upon their toes, on the alert.

FOREHAND POSITION

In a work which I have been doing with Dr. Schmidt, on "The Training of the Body" (Sonnenschein and Co.), it has been pointed out that exercises are easiest when each movement is a preparation for the next movement. Let us see the advantages of the above stroke from this point of view.

In (x) we saw that the body swings round forwards and towards the left: this would help to carry it into the forward-facing position (Position before and after a stroke, Illustration 10), and the change of the feet into the forward-facing position becomes very easy.

In (xii) we saw the racket "carried through" after the stroke: this would bring it naturally up towards the Hand-mirror position.

Thus, as the direct result of the Forehand stroke itself, we are partly prepared for the position which we ought to adopt after and before each stroke.

There is another possible position, in which the player may have his feet facing not sideways but forwards; but in this case he is apt to take the ball when it is not between him and the right hand Side-wall but when it is in front of him; he gets behind the ball and does most of the stroke with his wrist.

Now it is true that this may need less shifting of the feet, or rather that it may need a less unusual and more "natural" position of the feet, and that it gives the player the best possible view of the coming ball, i. e. the view from the point towards which it is coming. But it has too many disadvantages.

Not only is it almost impossible for a large number of strokes; but it is also a stroke that excludes that free and powerful body-swing along the line of the coming ball. It relies too much on a correct timing of the ball, and often on a mere flick of the wrist, which makes a very risky unreliable curve (as has been proved in the above-mentioned work).

But, whichever stroke be adopted, three things are certain.

1. The first is that the position must have been *already made* (grip correct, racket up and back, etc.) before the stroke is made. The stroke must not be made by the player while he is on the run.

2. The second is that the player must *keep his eye on the ball from the very moment that the ball has left the opponent's racket*. Till that time let him watch his opponent's eye or racket or arm; but after that time he must observe the golden rule of Golf.

3. The third is that, the moment the stroke is over, the player must be alert on his toes and

FOREHAND POSITION

prepared to have already got into position before he has to make the next stroke. Let him now look no longer at the ball but rather at his opponent.

When the simple stroke, the "Drive", has been mastered, it will be time enough to think of cutting or slicing the ball (i. e. of striking it not full but with the racket held at an angle), or of putting on a twist. The simple drive must also be mastered before the player tries to vary the pace or the direction, and before he tries to volley or half-volley. Here also the simple foundations must be firmly laid before the buildings be added.

The stroke is described elaborately in this Chapter: now the actual stroke at Squash will as a rule be somewhat shorter and sharper. But if the above stroke be practised assiduously (see Chapter VIII), the extra pace will soon come of its own accord.

CHAPTER VI.

BACKHAND POSITION AND STROKE.

THIS Chapter will be very much like the previous Chapter, *mutatis mutandis:* It will describe full and long strokes of an apparently elaborate character, in spite of the fact that the Squash stroke looks simple, when it is well done, and is in reality a short and quick stroke, as a general rule. But, if the beginner begins to practise correctly and slowly, he will soon find that the movements will be constantly becoming easier and easier, quicker and quicker.

We must assume that the correct Backhand grip has now become part and parcel of the player's personality. The grip need only be varied when the ball is to be taken high, e. g. in a Backhand volley. In this stroke the thumb may be moved up along the handle, so as to support the racket when it meets the ball. The Hand-mirror position, and the backward bending of the wrist towards the palm, must be observed here as carefully as in the Forehand stroke. Here, also, the grip must not be too tight before or after the stroke.

In this, even more than in the Forehand

BACKHAND POSITION 53

stroke, the Ball-game Apparatus will be of service, since by means of it the player can get a correct Backhand position and strike thousands of times in a very short while.

Let the player again think of his body as a clock, and his arm and racket as a pendulum of that clock. The body must not face the Front-wall: it must face sideways, so that the arm and racket will swing freely towards the Front-wall.

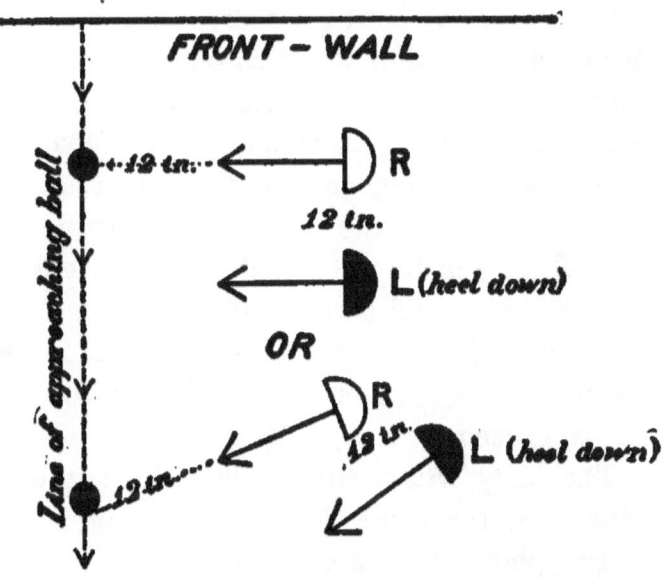

8. POSITION OF THE FEET FOR A BACKHAND STROKE.

The Illustration will show how the feet should be placed for a Backhand stroke, i. e. when the ball is coming to your left-hand side as you face towards the Front-wall. Personally I prefer the *second* (lower) position, as I find it gives a better swing; besides, as beginners usually err in having their feet in the waiting position (Illustration 10), they will find it will help them to exaggerate the opposite fault and to stand even further round than in the lower position.

There is another position of the feet which has the same advantages as the Forehand position mentioned above, viz, that they face more forwards; both are more " natural " and need less turning of the feet; both give a better sight of the ball. But both need more movement from place to place, and do not allow of a good swing, being mostly dependent on the lower arm (forearm) and on the wrist, which (see above) make risky and unreliable curves.

The feet should be as a rule about 12 inches apart, and the weight of the body should rest chiefly on the back or the left foot, before the stroke is made.

The body will naturally face the left hand Side-wall, since the feet are its foundations. If the player be taken unawares, and in the waiting position (Illustration 10), he should at any rate let his body face sideways, turning on the hips as on a pivot.

The face, however, must be turned towards the approaching ball, even while the body is

BACKHAND POSITION

turned well towards the left. The head should also be held up, i. e. with the chin back.

The left shoulder will be kept right back before the stroke: the left hand may be held up, as in Forehanders, if this is found to be a help.

Let the player now look at Illustration 9, and compare with it the following characteristics of the position before a Backhand stroke. Then let him put himself in this position, imagining a ball to be about 12 inches from the ground and about 12 inches in front of his right foot; or he can arrange a ball in this exact spot by means of the Ball-game Apparatus.

Throughout (i. e. both before and during the stroke).

(I) the feet face the right hand Side-wall, or are more round towards the Back-wall (right corner); the eye is kept on the ball.

Before the Stroke.

(II) the grip is correct;

(III) the racket is up and back to the left;

(IV) the wrist is bent forwards towards the palm:

(V) the left shoulder is back (the left hand may be held up);

(VI) the weight of body is on the back (left) foot.

During the Stroke.

(VII) the grip is tightened;

(VIII) the racket swings down and meets the low ball, to which it is all the time exposing its full face: the racket should swing away and out freely towards the left;

(IX) the wrist straightens itself (it may even bend away from the palm) as the ball is being struck; this adds pace;

(X) the body swings round forwards and towards the right, on the hips as on a pivot;

(XI) the weight of the body passes from the back foot (left) onto the front foot (right).

After the Stroke, notice once again the following points:—

(XII) the racket is carried through after the actual stroke: the left hand and arm may follow it. (Most Englishmen use their arms too little in skating as well as in these strokes);

(XIII) the racket then returns up to the Hand-mirror position;

(XIV) the wrist is now bent backwards again, away from the palm;

(XV) the body faces forwards.

(XVI) the weight of the body is evenly distributed between the two feet;

9. POSITION BEFORE A BACKHAND STROKE, EXAGGERATED

BACKHAND POSITION

(XVII) the two feet face forwards;

(XVIII) they rest upon their toes, on the alert.

This brings us to the positions and movements before and after strokes.

CHAPTER VII.

POSITIONS AND MOVEMENTS BEFORE AND AFTER STROKES.

WE have just seen the Forehand and Backhand positions and strokes, and how they should end up thus:—

(1) The racket is in the Hand-mirror position, the wrist being straight or perhaps bent backwards and towards the palms: this return to the Hand-mirror position is often extremely difficult, especially when a difficult or energetic stroke has thrown the player off his balance;

(2) the body rests its weight about equally between the two feet, which are, let us say, 12 inches apart; the body and the feet face forwards, and the feet rest not on the heels but on the toes. If the "keeping on the toes", ready to move either foot in one of several directions, proves difficult or tiring, this proves that practice is needed (see Chapter VIII).

The Illustration will show the waiting position before and after the Stroke. The exception will be when you are so sure that your opponent is going to hit say to your Forehand side and not to your Backhand; *then* you can

10. POSITION BEFORE AND AFTER A STROKE.
(WAITING POSITION.)

POSITIONS AND MOVEMENTS 59

remain facing as you are, if you are already in the Forehand position;

(3) the face of course faces forwards, as usual, half-watching the opponent if possible, i. e. looking towards the Front-wall in such a way that the opponent is dimly seen;

(4) alertness and readiness to anticipate the opponent's stroke and *to have moved into position* before the ball arrives—this is the keynote of the position before and after strokes, as distinct from the position and movements during strokes. This habit of being prompt and prepared to adapt oneself to the conditions, in a moment, will be of inestimable service not only in games and athletics, but also in every department of life and character.

(5) Exceptions similar to the above hold good of the next rule, that after a stroke you should return to a good position in the Court.

Which is the best position?

There are some who stay right forward between the Cross-line and the Front-wall, and volley everything; this exposes them to the opponent's stroke, and hardly seems to me to be quite fair. The opponent is not given free play to hit where he intends to. This position, however, is excellent practice for volleying, and may improve a Lawn-Tennis or Tennis (Court-Tennis) volley very noticeably.

For beginners, however, it is better to learr

the game off the floor first, i. e. to stand well back: so far back, indeed, that the racket in its swing will only just miss the Back-wall. The back foot might be about 4 feet from the Back-wall.

Whether this or a more forward spot be chosen, the spot must generally be near the centre line down the Court. To the spot, the base, the starting-point, the player should generally return after his stroke.

Directly you know whether the ball will come to your Forehand or to your Backhand

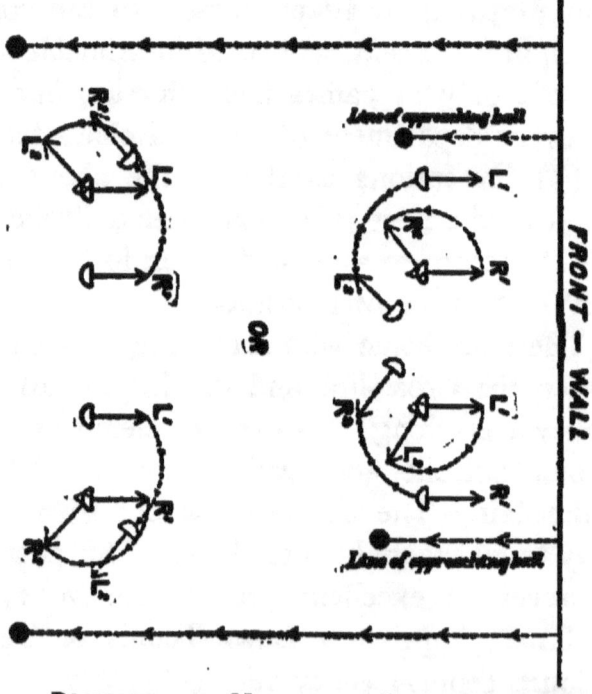

11. POSITIONS AND MOVEMENTS BEFORE STROKES.

POSITIONS AND MOVEMENTS

side, *immediately get into the Forehand or into the Backhand position*. Illustration 11 will show that there are two ways of doing this.

In the middle of the Illustration, you see your feet in the waiting position, resting on the toes.

(a) To get into the *Forehand* position, you may move your right foot back, so that it will be behind your left, and then turn your left foot round on its toe as a pivot. This will be better if the ball is to be taken far back in the Court.

(b) If, however, the ball is shorter and is to be taken rather more forward in the Court, then move your left foot *forward* and let your right foot rest on its toe. If the ball is to be taken very near where you are, you may move your left foot forward actually during the stroke itself.

Notice how either movement may help to bring the left shoulder forwards.

To move into the *Backhand* position from the waiting position, either

(a) move your left foot back and pivot your right foot round on its toe, or else

(b) move your right foot forward, and pivot your left foot round. Here, again, notice how either movement may help to draw *the left shoulder back*. The steps should be practised again and again until they have become quite easy and automatic: see Chapter VIII. I have practised them many thousands of times.

But, you will say, even if your feet are in the right Forehand or Backhand position, and your racket is up, and so on, it does not in the least follow that the ball will come to the right place.

This is true, but still *the right position, whether Forehand or Backhand, must first be formed and must then be kept*: this must be your first care. Having the feet in the right position, and resting on their toes, you can now move about the Court in this ready-made position. This is infinitely better than rushing to a ball and *then* changing into the position, if only because while you are rushing or directly after you have rushed you will find the change very hard to make. It will be almost bound to disconcert you.

It is needless to say that this sideway running is extremely awkward at first. But it will become easier and easier with practice, until at last you will be able to do as the result of conscious and repeated effort what Peter Latham, the Professional Racquet and Tennis Champion, does unconsciously and instinctively. Illustration 12 will suggest a few directions in which the feet may move: They must always preserve their relative positions.

POSITIONS AND MOVEMENTS 63

And these positions must have been formed as long as possible before the stroke is to be made.

Now it is a question whether one should move about with *short steps or with long*

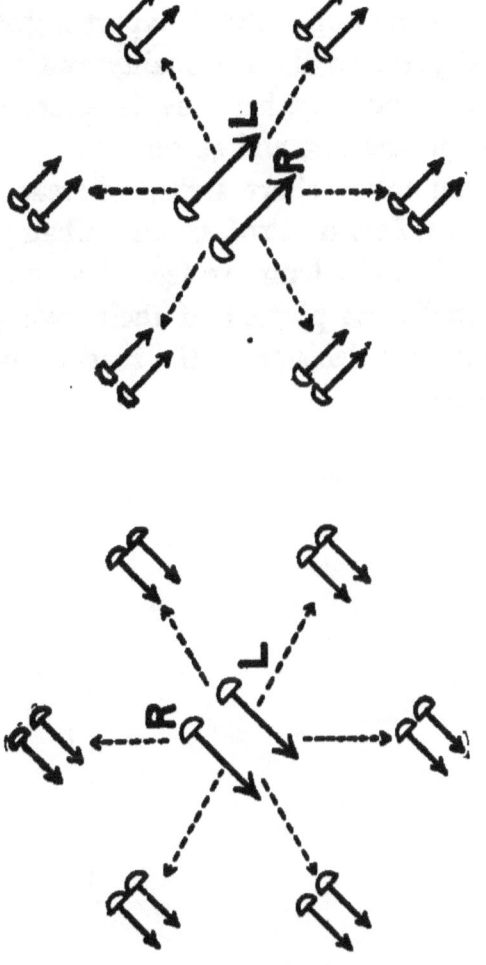

12. HOW TO MOVE TOWARDS A BALL.

strides. The former encourages the desirable habit of bright smartness, the latter the equally desirable habit of calmness and deliberateness. As to accuracy, there is little to choose between the two. It is possible that, with long strides, you will be less likely to be caught on the hop. But I expect a good deal might depend on the nationality and temperament, and on whether one is short or tall, lithe or ponderous, and so on.

Latham takes short steps, whereas Burke, the Lawn-Tennis Professional Champion of the world, takes long strides. I admire them both equally, as players of their own games; so I leave the decision to the reader's personal experience.

CHAPTER VIII.

PRACTICE OUTSIDE THE COURT.

IF the ideas suggested in the last Chapter are correct, then Squash is already proved to be a complex game. The ordinary beginner is very unlikely to do even the positions and movements *before* strokes in the right way. He is still more unlikely to do the strokes in the right way, even as single strokes. He is utterly unlikely to be able to think of all these many important points at once. In other words, the actual game of Squash is not the best way to learn Squash, *at first*. The Side-walls, the Back-walls, the various rapid motions of the ball, now here, and now there, distract the attention from the elementary positions and movements, which are the indispensable foundations of good play.

And therefore I suggest, as the result of a long personal experience, that any player who has the strength of will and the true ambition to improve, shall practise a great deal outside the Court. Few if any will have the grit and self-control to acquire the A B C of the game, to drill themselves thoroughly, in these elements before they go into a Court to play. But many will consent to practise *betweenwhiles*. And it is chiefly for these two classes of readers that I write these few hints. I can promise them that, if they once acquire the right positions and movements as an integral part of their personality, they will find their game improve rapidly but surely, and find it ever so much more interesting and instructive. Besides this, they will be able to teach others, for example their children or lady friends.

The habit of steady practice, when once acquired, will of itself be an invaluable possession. Such drudgery needs self-mastery, and in turn increases self-mastery and the vital power of concentrating the attention on the work in hand, as one might focus the sun's rays. Such work done in this way will never be regretted.

Let me take a concrete instance. Your Backhand stroke is weak, let us say for several reasons: e. g., you do not hold your racket up and back before the stroke begins, and your feet face forwards rather than sideways. But how can you correct these faults in the middle of the game, when you want to be thinking of where the next ball will come, where you will have to be, and where you will hit the ball when it does come? How can you concentrate your attention on one point, to say noth-

PRACTICE OUTSIDE THE COURT 67

ing of two or more points, when it is being distracted and divided now in this direction, now in that? Obviously, you cannot.

You need conditions where your attention will not be distracted or divided, but can be focussed and concentrated: you need to be where you can do just one thing at a time; you need to make just this one action a perfect, familiar, and almost automatic action, before you attack the second action. Or, to put it in another way, you need to use your brain-power so often upon this action that the action may at last be handed over to the Spinal Cord: it is thus that we have learnt to walk. That which was once directed by the will and the conscious effort of the brain is now directed almost automatically by the Spinal Cord. We want to be able to delegate as much work as we can to this useful apparatus, so that we may have our whole attention free to devote to the play and its tactics. We do not want to *be bothered with the mechanism of the play.*

Now, if you can go through various movements correctly and repeatedly, these will soon tend to become automatic. The more you concentrate your attention and energy and will upon the movement, the sooner it will become automatic.

But the attention cannot be concentrated on *complex* movements to start with: the movements must be simple. If a movement is complex, we must split it up into simple parts, and master these parts one by one.

What are these simple parts? We have already treated of the grip and the change of grip; the positions of the feet and the changes of position, including the sideway-running on the toes; and the Forehand stroke, and the Backhand stroke, including the movements of left shoulder, body, arm, wrist, and racket. And even this is very far from a complete list.

All these parts, which we have described above or shall describe below, should at first be taken one at a time, and repeated correctly and therefore at first slowly and with great care, and under healthy and favourable conditions which will not distract the mind.

These conditions will be described directly.

The grip has already been described in Chapter IV. It can easily be made to feel comfortable and natural, if only you will hold a racket or racket-handle in your hand e. g. while you read.

The Ball-game Apparatus will give still better practice not only in each single grip, but also in the change from one grip to the other. It would not be a bad idea to get a stick or umbrella with a handle shaped like a Squash racket handle: this would familiarise you with the correct grip, during a walk, without any

PRACTICE OUTSIDE THE COURT 69

expenditure of time or trouble. There are many players who have improved their play by doing imaginary strokes out-of-doors with ordinary walking-sticks.

The convenience of the racket handle (e. g. a broken racket cut short) cannot be overestimated: of course it has not the balance of weight, but it does for Squash players very much what the Harvard tank system does for rowing men: e. g. it makes the right grip of the handle feel perfectly natural. The rackethandle can be used in rooms where a racket could not be safely used, and it can be carried in a bag in which a racket could not be carried at all.

It gives a good "excuse" for a little exercise the first thing in the morning and the last thing at night.

The Foot-positions and Foot-movements have also been described, in Chapters V, VI, and VII. The movements on p. 62 should be repeated, at first slowly and carefully, until they have become almost as easy as the movements of walking. The places for the feet should be marked on the floor with chalk.

Here again the Ball-game Apparatus will be valuable. Let the ball be about 12 inches from the ground and 12 inches from you. Then move away from it and, keeping your eye intent on the ball, move into position (either by strides or by short steps, see above). Then look down on the floor to see if you are standing correctly.

The exercises would be as follows:

Waiting-position to Forehand position; vice versa;

waiting to Backhand; vice versa;

Forehand to Backhand; vice versa;

Forehand to Forehand in another place;

Backhand to Backhand;

waiting position to Forehand in another place;

waiting position to Backhand in another place.

In all these exercises, move about on the toes, with the head facing forwards, the chin back, the racket in the Hand-mirror position, and the wrist bent backwards away from the palm before the Forehand stroke, but forwards towards the palm before the Backhand stroke.

It is good practice simply to move about in all directions on the toes. This is extremely useful for other purposes besides the game of Squash, e. g. even for walking in the street or road.

The Strokes.

Parts of the stroke have already been practised, viz, the grip, and the foot-positions and movements. The movements of body-turn-

13. (a) TURNING ON THE HIPS.

PRACTICE OUTSIDE THE COURT

ing on the hips, of weight-shifting from leg to leg, of arm, and of wrist, still remain to be acquired one by one. About the finger-movements we shall not say much in this little book.

The body-turnings on the hips have been described in "Lessons in Lawn-Tennis" (Upcott Gill & Co., London, Scribner's, New York). They are very like some of the Health-Exercises of the Swedish Gymnastics: in fact, they are excellent not only for the litheness of the body, but also as a help against indigestion and constipation. By bringing into use some of the strongest and largest muscles of the body, they give better exercise for the heart, they improve the circulation, and they induce less fatigue: if they are done rhythmically (e. g. while you hum a tune) they will produce still less fatigue, as we have pointed out in the "The Training of the Body". Besides these merits, the body-turnings are almost indispensable for many Ball-Games, e. g. for Golf and Cricket, as well as for boxing and wrestling, Putting the Weight or Shot, Throwing the Hammer, and so on.

It may be better to begin with the hands on the hips and the heels together, the feet being at right angles to one another. Holding the chin back, turn on your hips round to the left (not far enough to produce a strain), and then back again. Do this a good many times.

Then go to the right similarly. Then go from right to left and from left to right. The distance will naturally increase as your joints and muscles get into working order.

Next, stand with your feet about 12 inches apart, and face forwards. Then shift the weight of the body from the left foot to the right, and back again, several hundred times.

Then, keeping the same position of the feet, bend first one leg and then the other, in many directions, letting the weight of the body pass from one leg to the other.

Then, keeping your chin back all the time, turn your neck slowly round first to one side and then to the other, and then up and down, and so on. This is a useful exercise to try while walking, or sitting or waiting in a car or train.

A still more useful *Neck-exercise* is to keep the face facing forwards constantly in the same direction, while you do the body-turnings described above.

The *Arm-Exercises* are easy to devise. First the whole arm can be moved in a pendulum-swing; then the forearm can be moved up and down, the arm above the elbow being kept quite rigid.

The *Wrist-Exercises* are still more important. I should suggest that they should be first practised with the hand open, rather than

13. (b) TURNING ON THE HIPS.

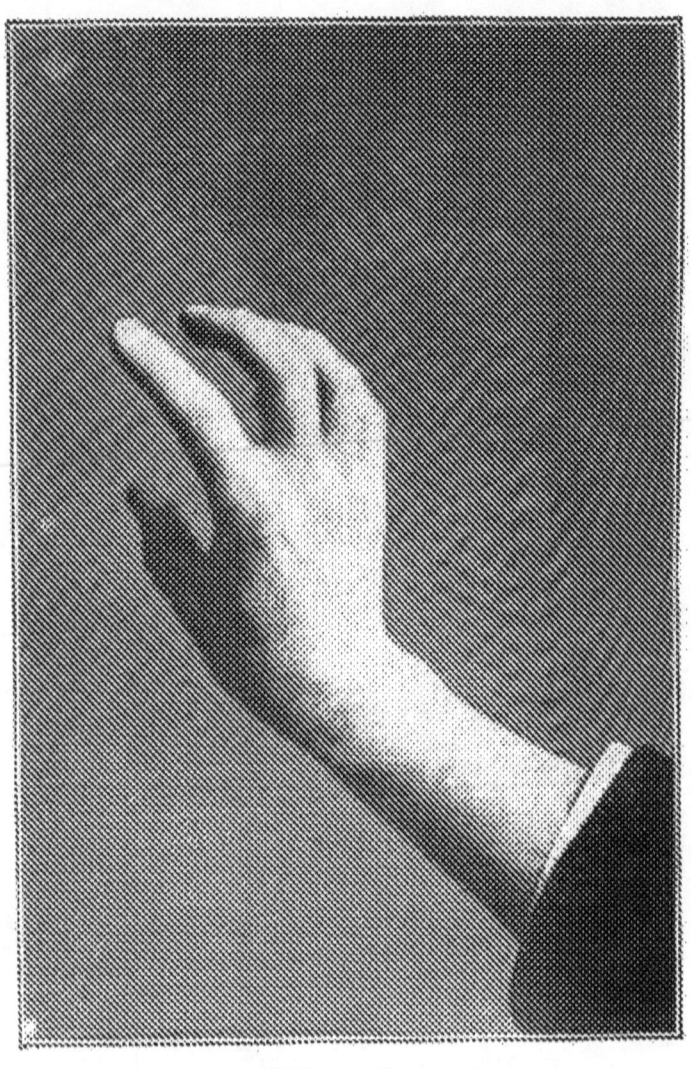

14. (a) WRIST-EXERCISE.

PRACTICE OUTSIDE THE COURT 73

with the tightened grip. This will give more suppleness and pace.

These are just two out of many possible examples. Hold the hand as in (a), and then move the outer edge (the little finger) down and round to the left, and the inner edge (the thumb) up and round to the right, till the hand is as it is in (b). Then reverse the movement. There are many strokes where this turn is of great importance. Another would be to hold the hand with its back towards you, the hand up as far as it will go, in the direction of the shoulder, and then let it move down as far as it will go.

When each one of these parts has been acquired *per se*, then two should be combined, until the two together have been acquired; to these a third can be added, and so on, until eventually the whole position and movement before and during and after the strokes has been mastered part by part.

But, as in the conquest of Italy by the Romans, so here, each part must be thoroughly won, and all the parts that have been won must be consolidated and made to co-operate harmoniously, before a new part be attacked.

Actual games of Squash are excellent: nothing can quite take their place, either for recreation and enjoyment, or for social intercourse. And such exercises as I have suggested involve much self-denial and drudgery. But I have already given one or two reasons why such exercises are really worth while; and let me now give a few more reasons as well.

The exercises are simple and easy, and all beginnings ought to be simple and easy. It is on exactly the same principle that I should urge people to begin by learning Squash before they attempt to learn Tennis (Court-Tennis) or Racquets.

They are cheap and need a very small space and very little apparatus: many of them need no apparatus at all. They can be practised anywhere and at any time of the year, season, or day, and for just a few minutes together. They are thus an excellent way of using up *odd moments,* e. g., between work- or business-hours, or just after rising or before going to bed, or while one is waiting. They need no opponent, and no instructor; if no one is near to correct you, you can correct yourself by standing in front of a looking-glass.

Though not the ideal form of recreation, still they are a recreation, and most of them are positively healthy.

Aesthetically, they improve the carriage of the body and increase its ease and grace of movement.

Practically, they give you more control of

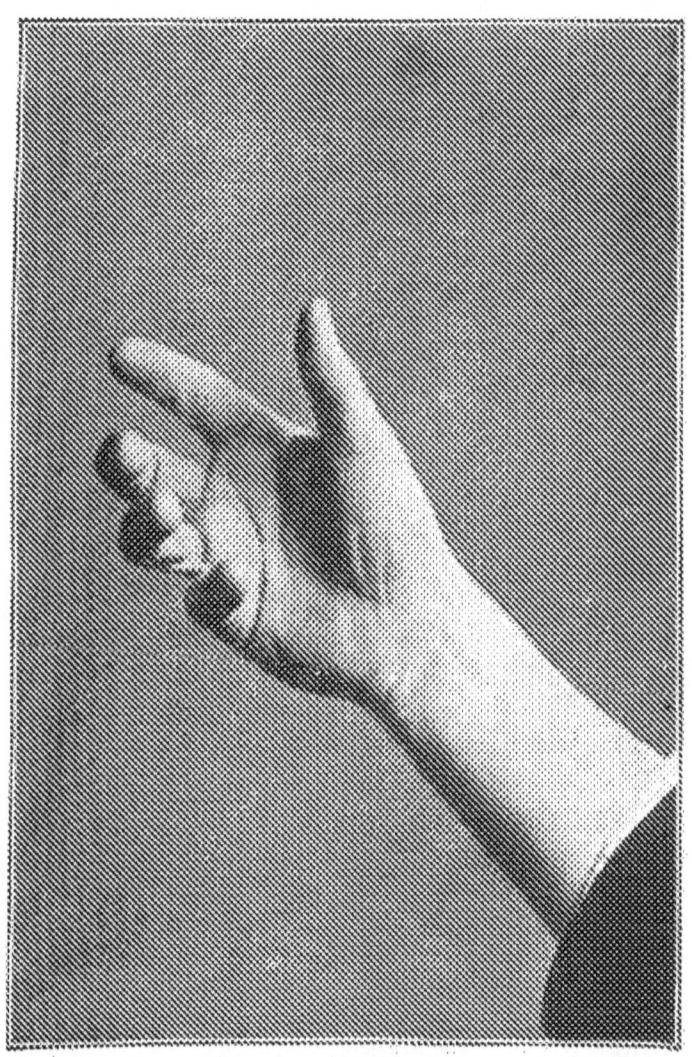

14. (b) WRIST-EXERCISE.

PRACTICE OUTSIDE THE COURT 75

the limbs, and form the foundations of many of the best games and forms of athletics. They make the whole self active and prompt, and yet calm and patient.

In themselves they are interesting, not only because they illustrate the scientific way of learning or teaching *anything whatsoever*, but also because they may improve your game almost day by day, and give you the best possible chance of correcting your faults. You would be scarcely likely to correct them *en masse*. And, in proportion as your game improves, your enjoyment of it is bound to increase also.

As to the improvement, I can safely answer for it in the case of myself and of many other players who have learnt the system. It is only at first that little or no fruit appears.

The theoretical objector will say that these movements are so elaborate and need such careful attention that they will make the stroke conscious and ponderous and slow. The exact reverse is nearer to the truth. Correct practice and repetition, done with careful attention, will make the stroke as unconscious as walking, and as neat and fast as running. It is a law of nature that he who repeats the same action again and again, consciously, will eventually be able (nay he may be forced to) to do it almost or quite unconsciously, having turned the "voluntary" movement into what may be called an artificial instinct.

The piano-player, the writer, the typewriter, the cyclist, may begin slowly and carefully: but it does not follow that this slowness and carefulness will make the movement slow and will necessitate care say a year hence.

And indeed for most people, if not for the genius-players who are few and far between, unless a thing be at first done correctly, slowly, and consciously, it will never be done *correctly*, quickly, and sub-consciously or unconsciously. The pace will increase of itself and the effort which is required will decrease.

If it be urged that few will take the trouble, or that the practice is not worth the while, I have little to answer: I write for those who want to improve and to do themselves justice. I offer them the best advice I can. If it is not worth while to improve, it is hardly worth while to be a player at all. At least I think so. As to the idea of such practice spoiling the pleasure of the game, and turning the game into slavery, this is just precisely what it does *not* do. It is not itself a pleasure, but it does add to the pleasure of the game, as my friends Mr. T. Suffern Tailer and Mr. Hubert Higgins would gladly testify. And it adds to the pleasure of many other games as well.

PRACTICE OUTSIDE THE COURT

They will also bear me out when I say that the game is not a simple game which anyone can play well, a game which needs no learning and no practice. It is at least as complex as most games, or rather it can be made so, if it be played properly.

You think, perhaps, that the "natural" way of playing must be the best? You are right, *if* the "natural" way is also the correct way. It was not so in my own case, and it is so in very, very few cases. I had to unlearn almost everything that I did "naturally", and learn the game again part by part. *I have never regretted the trouble I took,* e. g. the thousands of movements I practised nearly every morning.

It is equally wrong to suppose that "Practice makes perfect". Practice in wrong habits makes a person less and less likely to become perfect: it gives him so much to unmake before he can hope to make the correct movements successfully; to repeat the incorrect movements, again and again, tends to turn them into unconscious habits, into parts of the player himself. Habit and repetition must work these movements into the very fibres of his being.

Or, you may say, "A duffer will never improve." You are right: he is never likely to improve so long as he is never taught or else is taught by some one who does the stroke rightly without in the least knowing why or how. I believe that any duffer, so long as he has any sort of an " eye ", can improve at this game if only he will take the trouble to drill himself in the A B C of the game.

I know that many readers will object and say that I have told them a great deal that they knew already. But I am writing principally not for good players so much as for beginners and for those who may want to teach others. Besides this, I could not decide exactly what a given reader does know already; under such conditions I thought it safer to give too much than to give too little.

But great care must be taken to ensure the best conditions. If you cannot or do not care to practise in the open air, then the windows of the room must be open at the top and bottom. The barer the room, the fewer things there are in it to distract your attention, (except of course the Ball-Apparatus), the easier and quicker the progress will be.

(2) Rhythmical movement of the large muscles is far less tiring than irregular movement. Thus the large muscles of the heart can work prodigiously, because they work rhythmically. But even rhythmical movements must at last produce fatigue, and it is important to

stop any exercise before the fatigue-point is reached.

You can either rest, or change the exercise. A few exercises, each done many times, are better than either one exercise done till it has become quite monotonous, or many exercises each done once or twice.

(3) While exercising throw your whole attention, your whole will, into the movements and their correctness: let the mind move into the muscles.

(4) As a help to this, think less of the present drudgery and more of the future gain, being assured that, if you do this work with a will now, you will not have to think of it at all afterwards. *Prospice finem.*

(5) Keep records (e. g. in a note-book) of the number of exercises done in a given time, of the improvement, and so on. This also will make the practice less like slavery.

In conclusion, let me repeat once more:—

Make as much as possible already automatic and instinctive, and delegate to the Spinal Cord, that wonderful time-saving apparatus, as much as possible of the correct movements and positions of the game *before you begin even to practise* in the Court, but anyhow before you play actual games at all frequently.

And, when you have begun to play games frequently, exercise and correct—

(a) your weak points in friendly games;

(b) your still weaker points in practice *inside* the Court;

(c) your weakest points (e. g. the positions of your feet) in practice outside the Court.

CHAPTER IX.

PRACTICE INSIDE THE COURT.

It would be best not to begin to practise with a racket and ball inside the Court until the elementary positions and movements have become easy and natural. I will assume that these have become easy and natural, and that the player now has a good position and a good stroke, (i. e. a stroke made up of many good parts well combined and consolidated). Let him now go into the Squash-Court *by himself:* this would be less likely to distract him than if he went in with anyone else, even with a teacher. I may mention here that these remarks about practice inside the Court are meant to apply also to the " Knock-up " before the game begins.

In practising inside the Court, let him have the same aim that he has already had in practising outside the Court, viz. to make as much as possible automatic and certain before he plays the actual game. It will therefore be necessary for him to take various strokes one by one, and to begin by doing them slowly, and under *easy conditions*, until they have become a second instinct. Similarly, in English Billiards, one ought to make absolutely certain not only of the correct holding of the cue, but also of the ordinary strokes (e. g. the stroke into the end-pocket off the red ball); for one knows that *some* of these are almost sure to be offered in the course of the game. It is chiefly by making some of the easy common strokes a dead certainty that the professional so often beats the amateur.

(1) Before you actually hit the ball, throw it up against the Front-wall and *notice where it falls at its second bounce*: for in the game you will have to hit the ball only just before this, if you possibly can.

(2) After watching the second bounce of a number of balls off the Front-wall, try moving into position, so that the second bounce shall be about 12 to 18 inches from your two feet. Notice whether your tendency is to get too near the ball, or too far forward (this is the commonest error), or too far behind; and correct yourself accordingly.

(3) The Ball-Game Apparatus has given you a large number of strokes of precisely the same kind, in succession. Now try a number of strokes of a somewhat similar kind in succession, first Forehand and then Backhand. Throw the ball up, and then make the single

PRACTICE INSIDE THE COURT 83

stroke, after having got into the right position: for this should have been easy owing to the practice in (2). After each stroke, let the racket come up to the Hand-mirror position.

(4) Then do several strokes in succession, taking the Forehand first. Stand in the Forehand position, a little behind the place where the dividing line and the cross-court line meet, and try to return the ball against the Frontwall between yourself and the right hand Sidewall. You will have to move backwards or forward, or to the one side or the other or obliquely, in order that the ball may be just right for you, i. e. in order that it be about 12 to 18 inches from your two feet and about 12 inches from the ground when you strike it. But always move about (as in Illustration 12, p. 63) all ready in the Forehand position, with the racket up and back. Be on the spot *before* the ball has arrived. Don't wait to start till the ball has already bounced once. Keep on your toes the whole time.

Before and during the stroke, watch the ball persistently, and begin to watch it again as soon as you can after the stroke. Sometimes you will be compelled to hit the ball when it is too near you, or else when it is high in the air. It is only the majority of strokes that you will be able to hit in the ideal position.

Above all, hit the ball out and away from

you; not onto the Side-wall first, however, but towards the right-hand corner of the Front-wall. If you find that you are hitting across, towards the left-hand corner, look down at your feet, and you will probably find them out of position. Correct accordingly, or even exaggerate the opposite fault.

If you are hitting across, when you want to hit down the side, your feet are probably facing forwards too much. If you are hitting *too high*, your feet are probably *too far behind* the ball; if too low, your feet are probably too far in front of the ball.

After the stroke, move back at once to the central position (just behind the cross-line).

As soon as this return has become easy, say 10 times in succession, for the Forehand stroke, try to reach the same stage with the Backhand stroke, going through the same process *mutatis mutandis*.

Begin the Forehand and Backhand strokes, slowly: the pace will naturally increase itself. Begin them also with the full face of the racket, so as to present the largest possible surface to the ball.

(5) Then begin meeting the ball with the racket held at an angle, so as to slice or cut the ball. This will be useful not only for a change stroke, but also as a preparation for Tennis (Court-Tennis) and for the service at

15. POSITION IN WAITING FOR A BALL OFF THE BACK-WALL.

PRACTICE INSIDE THE COURT 85

Racquets and for an occasional stroke at Lawn-Tennis.

(6) Not until you have thoroughly mastered both Forehand and Backhand strokes down the Side-walls, should you try the stroke across the Court from side to side. This will need a rapid change of the position from the Forehand to the Backhand, as well as the movements backwards or forwards or sideways. Don't forget to finish with the racket up after each stroke.

(7) When this exercise has become easy, try it with a cut.

(8) *The Back-wall* will be the next study. To have learnt the angles will be most useful for Tennis (Court-Tennis) and Racquets, but not for Lawn-Tennis unless a Court with a Back-wall ever be adopted.

Here, again, do not begin by hitting the ball, but first *face the Back-wall,* and throw the ball up full against the Back-wall several times and notice where it falls at its second bounce.

Then do the same, but also get into position, i. e. so that the second bounce will be about 12 to 18 inches from your feet.

Now at last try the stroke itself, keeping on your toes until you have got into position: of course your racket will be up. Practise this till you get the Forehand stroke easy, then try the Backhand stroke.

Next you should throw the ball onto the floor before it hits the Back-wall: after first noticing the angle, and then getting into position, practise the strokes themselves. You will have to be sharper here, since the ball has already bounced once.

Now face the right-hand corner of the Back-wall, and throw some balls into this right-hand corner. First notice the second bounce, then get into position, then practise the strokes. As before, first acquire the stroke where the ball hits the corner full, and then the stroke where it hits the floor before it goes into the corner.

Acquire the Backhand strokes of the left-hand corner of the Back-wall in just the same way.

You will find that the strokes up to this point are very similar. The downward swing of the racket meets the low ball with its full face, and then carries through the stroke and ends up with the Hand-mirror position.

(9) The *Service* may be taken next.

First hit the ball, fair and square and without any cut, at some spot just above the higher (or Service) line on the Front-wall; do this until you can be sure of hitting or nearly hitting the spot. Look at the spot before you begin, but look at the ball directly your arm commences to move. At least this seems to be

16. POSITION BEFORE THE FOREHAND SERVICE.

PRACTICE INSIDE THE COURT

a better plan, for most people, than to keep the eye on the spot all the time.

Correct the direction or elevation, not so much by your wrist, as (a) by the angle of your feet, and (b) by the place to which you throw the ball. That is to say, if you were hitting too much to your left, let your body (and its feet or pedestals) face more towards your right. If you are hitting too low, then throw the ball further in front of you.

When these services have become easy, increase the pace; then practise them with a cut.

The Backhand Service, from the left-hand side of the Court, is of the greatest value not only as a change Service, but also for Racquets. I have occasionally found it useful in Tennis (Court-Tennis).

A twist Service, Forehand and Backhand, might perhaps be added to your stock-in-trade.

It is good to be able to send *all* these Services so that they will pitch in the 'nick' (i. e. where the Side-wall meets the floor) at various parts of the Side-wall. This will immediately give you the advantage in a rally.

Last of all, you must learn to be equally accurate with the Service at whatever pace you send it, and you must be able to vary the pace at will.

(10) The *Volley* must be learnt, but it should not be learnt until the stroke off the ground has been mastered.

The general rules as to grip and position and movements are very similar, except that the grip must often be somewhat tighter, and nearer to the face of the racket, and the wrist stiffer, and the stroke slower, meeting the ball rather than smashing it. The racket slowly advances along the line of the approaching ball; for the sake of change, the racket sometimes is held almost still, or even retires from the approaching ball.

The Volley is often more unreliable than the ordinary stroke; but (a) it is sometimes the only resource left; (b) it saves one's energy, by saving the run backwards; (c) it takes the opponent by surprise; (d) it is good practice, especially for Lawn-Tennis.

Very much the same will apply to the Half-Volley, the most graceful stroke in the game, and the most satisfactory—when it comes off.

It is usually too risky, however, since a step forwards will turn it into a Volley, which is easier, and a step backwards will turn it into an ordinary stroke. It must be remembered also, that Squash, as opposed to Racquets and to some extent to Tennis (Court-Tennis), is pre-eminently a safety game.

17. POSITION BEFORE THE BACKHAND SERVICE.

In the Half-Volley it is even more fatal to smash at the ball than in the full Volley. In the Half-Volley, the stroke is seldom carried through quite so far: it is sometimes cut shorter, as in some approach-strokes at Golf.

CHAPTER X.

THE GAME ITSELF, AND ITS TACTICS.

We come at last to the game itself, having first acquired the correct positions and movements (as the would-be swimmer might before he tried to swim), and having then tested them and practised them alone in the Squash-Court, where failures are unimportant and faults easy to correct (as the would-be swimmer might swim and still keep within his depth).

Before the game itself begins, it is usual and useful to have a short " Knock-up ", so as to get the muscles and nerves and eye into working order, and to get accustomed to the bounce of the ball and the light of the Court. This " Knock-up ", which is a special branch of " Practice inside the Court " (Chapter VII), should itself be preceded by one or two of the chief Exercises in " Practice outside the Court " (Chapter VII), though there will generally be very little time.

At the beginning of the " Knock-up " you might remember to let the ball bounce a few times without hitting it: this gives you a far better idea of the requirements than if you were to try to hit the ball right at the start.

When the hitting does begin, let it be at first very gentle. In the Inter-Public-School Matches at the Queen's Club, West Kensington, I often used to notice boys begin the " Knock-up " with a series of the very hardest drives just above the line. This is altogether wrong.

When you knock-up, notice in what ways and for what reasons (p. 84) you are playing wrongly, e. g. too high, too low, or too much across the Court; and correct accordingly. And begin not only correctly and slowly, but also with strokes down the Side-walls (p. 85), rather than across the Court: the latter strokes are so easy to add when once the game is in full swing.

During the first game you have to try to harmonise two principles.

(1) You must play for safety, waiting for your opponent to miss a ball, or gradually getting him out of position, but not trying to kill all the ordinary balls that come. You should lead up to a killing stroke, just as you should do in Lawn-Tennis: for instance, get your opponent to the front of the Court, and then send a stroke which will *just* reach the Back-wall.

In accordance with this principle of safety,

hit the ball low, but not too low: a good plan is to have an *imaginary* tell-tale a few inches above the real tell-tale, just as some Lawn-Tennis players play with an imaginary net in their mind's eye.

Gradually increase the pace and the general severity of your stroke, as you warm to your work: but it is not bad to keep something " up your sleeve ", at least with certain opponents. I have often won a Tennis Match by keeping a special service in reserve till the critical moment.

The last stroke of all to be resorted to is the inelegant stroke onto the Side-wall. It can be used in an emergency, but perpetually to bang the Side-wall instead of hitting down the Side-wall is very very bad practice, besides spoiling the game not a little. It pays with a beginner, in the sense that it scores aces, but it develops a rather bad style.

As you warm to your work, you can also vary the pace, hitting now with your body-swing and arm-swing and forearm-movement and wrist-flick, all together, now with two or more of these.

(2) The second principle is *to try a needless variety of strokes near the beginning* of the game, so as to ascertain your opponent's strong and weak points, as well as your own, on this particular day: having found your op-

ponent's weak points, you can give him plenty of practice in strengthening them!

But this plan of feeling your way may be fatal unless you can keep cool and calm: for it may lose you the first game and give your opponent confidence. Much will depend on your own nature and on that of your opponent. During the game, as during the "Knock-up", try to find out the cause of your faults, and exaggerate the opposite faults: thus glance to see whether your feet are facing too much forwards, and see if your racket is up before and after each stroke.

One of the commonest faults is to stand too near the Front-wall; you often have to volley or half-volley, and do not get enough of the best strokes, viz. those which are near the second bounce. Nine beginners out of ten get too near the ball, so that it is too close to their side and a real swing is impossible. They also take it too soon, while it is too far in front of them, and too high in the air.

A second fault, which is still commoner than the first, is the habit of *standing on the heels before and after strokes,* the habit of getting glued to the ground, or, as they say admirably in Devonshire, "stugged".

Thus a player often completely collapses after his stroke, especially if it has been an effort or if it has resulted in a good low drive.

He ought to assume that the ball *will* be returned if it *can* be returned. He ought to be on the alert, on his toes, directly after he has hit the ball.

This almost incessant moving and moving on the toes is apt to be very tiring. In " The Training of the Body " (Sonnenschein and Co.) we have shown how much of the exertion of walking and running consists in raising the weight of the body on the toes. In Squash and in Racquets and in Tennis (Court-Tennis) it is only a splendid " eye ", superb judgment, and prolonged experience, that can in any way make up for the fault of standing on the heels.

And so it follows that the ordinary player should be in training (see Chapter IX.). This if done properly, will also help him to keep his temper calm and patient.

But, with all this calmness and patience, *the player should play up almost or quite his hardest throughout the game,* except (see above) just at the very start.

How, then, can we manage to get a good even game with a weaker or slacker player? This is one of the chief problems in all forms of competition: how can it be arranged that the stronger shall have to do his level best to keep ahead of, nay even to keep up with, the weaker?

Regular Handicaps are the best help: I do

THE GAME AND ITS TACTICS 95

not mean mere points (e. g. 10 points in each Game), but such Handicaps as will be suggested in Chapter XI. (e. g. "Half-the Court", "No Volleying", "Only Volleying", and so on).

But what if the opponent refuses?

Then there are several remedies.

(1) I should suggest a fine of a shilling or 25 cents, to be paid to the Club (or to the opponent's credit account at the Club) by anyone who shall not have reached more than a certain number of points (say 7) at the end of the game. The marker should be asked to arrange the Handicap.

(2) If ever the weaker player is so idiotic and selfish as to refuse the proper odds, then, unless you altogether decline to play with him, *voluntarily* dock off one or more of your strongest points. This will give you self-control. Are you good at volleying? Then cease to volley. Are you good at placing? Then cease to place;

(3) or, rather, try to place balls so that your opponent shall be able to get them without moving. This will give you not only control of yourself but also control of the ball: for you must have control of it if you can hit it just wherever you like.

It is a great error to suppose that you must necessarily weaken your game by playing with an inferior player. By this means you could strengthen it amazingly.

(4) Or you can make experiments and *tours de force*. But, as a rule, it is better to practise your weaker or weakest points against an inferior opponent: for, if you do not succeed in the brilliant *tour de force*, the rally certainly stops; whereas, if you *do* succeed, the rally probably stops also, since your opponent fails to return the ball. And the long rallies are among the chief merits and charms of Squash.

We noted above that a splendid "eye" and superb judgment and prolonged experience make up for many faults. The "eye" (which means a rapid sympathy between eye, nerve, and hand, rather than good sight) may be trained e. g. by manual work like carpentering; the judgment may be trained e. g. by constant speculation as one watches players, and a mental registry of the result. But merely to see, merely to judge, these are not enough. And it is not enough merely to have had a prolonged experience: there must have been also careful observation made, and record must have been kept, and the points observed must have been carried out in practice.

For example, there are many who have played hundreds of games of Squash, and who still do not know whether the average opponent is most likely, nay almost certain, to return the ball: they will not observe and remember and act accordingly. One man told me that he never could take a certain service at Tennis: I watched him trying to take it, and I noticed that the service always had a certain twist, and always came off the Back-wall at about the same angle, and that my friend always expected it to come off at another angle!

CHAPTER XI.

HANDICAPS.

IN the previous Chapter, Handicaps were not mentioned. At the present time they are little used, at least the best Handicaps are little used; and this is one reason why so many people have thought Squash to be a monotonous Game of " Smack-ball ", a game which requires no skill; just as so many people have thought Lawn-Tennis to be a monotonous Game of " Pat-ball ".

Most men have had a very hazy and incorrect idea as to what a Handicap should be and do: they expect that it shall produce a game with the *points* fairly level, and of course this is one of the chief functions of a Handicap. But it should also have other functions, which are far more valuable.

It should produce a game that is worth seeing, a game of long rallies, for example. I have seen a Handicap game that was very even so far as actual points were concerned: but the server at one time served off ten points running. The spectators had no pleasure and little help from the sight.

HANDICAPS

Nor was it only for the spectators that the game was without pleasure and without help: of the two players themselves (the parties chiefly concerned) the stronger got next to no practice: he was able to kill the ball time after time when it came to him; but too few balls came to him. He never had to exert himself "all round". *To the stronger player the Handicap should give practice, not only in a mere safety game,* but also in

(I) developing and improving his weakest points (e. g. his Backhand strokes); and in

(II) teaching him to get control of the ball, especially by being compelled to place it accurately; and in giving his stroke

(III) variety of pace and direction etc.

Both players should be compelled to play up throughout if they wish to win.

The weaker player, according to the ordinary system of Handicaps by mere points, finds that he gets few balls that he can return: the rallies are short, and his best strokes do not receive their due: the stronger player returns them easily. Thus the weaker player gets little real practice, and is much discouraged.

Or, if the stronger player obviously hits every ball to the weaker player, the latter is apt to be either insulted or else disheartened. I know of one good player who stands near the middle of the Court and returns practically every ball, whether hard or easy, with the greatest facility. The opponent thus has none of the satisfaction of making a good stroke.

The weaker player should find that the Handicap gives him

(I) plenty of fairly easy balls, and, if possible, balls of more or less the same kind, e. g. Backhanders far back in the Court, and balls which he can return;

(II) encouragement, partly through the satisfaction of seeing a good stroke win a point.

We have now said something of what Handicaps should really be and do. And, if to these important functions the reader adds the social function, the power of bringing together, in a friendly and interesting game, people whose standards of play are ever so far apart, he will surely be ready to give a fair trial to any new suggestion. But he may doubt if Handicaps can really achieve all this.

Let us see what Handicaps can be added to the Handicaps by points and *bisques* (a *bisque* being a point to be taken at will), so that the former may be used in addition to or instead of the latter.

In the following pages, A will stand for the stronger player, B for the weaker.

HANDICAPS

(1) *The Handicap by points or bisques* is simple: but the bisque is practically unnecessary in Squash.

A gives B, as a start, a certain number of aces, so that, for example, B may start the game at 10-0.

A owes so many aces; thus, if he owes 10, he has to score 10 points before he reaches 0. At one stage of the game the score might be "(A) owe 8, (B) 1". This gives a longer game.

Let me here recommend *the Handicaps that rise or fall according to the result of each game.* If B says that the game should be even, that A cannot give him odds, then let the Rising or Falling Handicap system be adopted. Let the first game be even: if B wins, well and good; but, if B loses, then let A give one ace; if B loses again, let A give 2 aces, and so on. Only let the Handicap for each new game depend on the result of the last game, whether that last game be a week ago or just a few moments ago. If, when B receives 10, he beats A, then he goes down to 9.

In each Club there should be, as at Golf, a list of members classed by points. Monthly competitions might alter a man's class.

(2) A good Handicap is to play with the ordinary rules (Chap. II.), but to *let the*

weaker (B) score every point that he wins: i. e., if he wins a rally, he scores an ace, as well as putting himself in.

(3) A can give B two or more Services (or innings or hands) instead of only one.

(4) A can play with some *special implement*, e. g. a Court-Tennis racket, a small flat stick, etc. The smaller implement will necessitate greater accuracy and care, especially in the position and timing of the ball. The weaker player will get more easy balls to return.

A may be obliged to use his two hands: this will give him fine exercise, compelling him not only to use the left arm etc., but also to stoop. He may (see below) have his Volley prohibited.

(5) Or he may be obliged to catch the ball and then throw it; or to go through some movement (e. g. to touch the floor with his left hand) before each stroke.

(6) Left-handed play with some sort of racket is good for a change, and for the health and development of the body. We are apt to be one-sided in our development. Left-handed play teaches us the importance of a correct position (including the Hand-mirror position). It gives the weaker player plenty of balls to return and to kill.

HANDICAPS 103

(7) If A is weak on his Backhand side, let him be compelled to take every ball backhanded.

(8) Let A be obliged to leave every ball to hit the floor. *A Volley shall count as a miss.* This will improve his Back-wall play as well as his ordinary stroke, and it will compel him to half-volley or else to move rapidly on his feet. The weaker player is given more time to recover and to get into position.

(9) The reverse of this, where *only the Volley counts as a stroke,* is an exceptionally hard game, but the best possible practice for Lawn-Tennis.

(10) Let A play the game called " No Sidewalls ", i. e., if any stroke of his shall hit the Side-wall, it shall count against him. By this latter is meant a Stroke which either

(i) falls onto the Side-wall, before it has bounced, or else

(ii) (11) falls onto the Side-walls while still in play (i. e. before it has bounced twice).

The same applies to

(12) *" Touch-no-walls ".*

All of these give the stronger player more control of the ball; and give the weaker player more easy balls to get and to punish.

(13) If A be obliged (i) to hit every ball above the *Service line,* he is encouraged in a

weak style; it is better to limit his strokes to (ii) the Front-wall between the higher or Service-line and the play-line or Tell-tale.

(14) (i) When A wishes to practise placing, both down the sides and across the Court, and when B wishes to practise e. g. Back-hand play, then let A give "*Half-the-Court*". Each stroke of his must bounce say in the left-hand half of the Court.

(ii) Or A may have to confine his balls to the two front sections, or to one of them, or to the two back sections or to one of them. The section may be changed at the beginning of a new game.

(15) (i) *The Lawn-Tennis Scoring* has been described. It prevents a man from serving off too many aces in quick succession.

(16) And so does my system by which *each player is allowed two Services*, no more and no less, one from each Court. Each point counts as an ace.

(17) Many of the above Handicaps can be *combined* with one another or with the Handicap by points. Thus a very much stronger player, A, might give B 10 points and "Touch-no-Side-walls" and might play with his hands.

(18) Two fairly even players will do well to exchange Handicaps. Let one confine himself to Backhanders and receive 7 aces; or let

HANDICAPS

one play "No Volleying" while the other plays "Only Volleying".

(19) The importance of *self-imposed or voluntary Handicaps* has been already pointed out.

(20) Other Handicaps might be devised by any one who gave a little time to the question. Tennis (Court-Tennis) has a more complete system than any other game.

In conclusion, let B, the receiver of the Handicap, remember that he must risk more: he who receives most must risk most.

CHAPTER XII.

GENERAL HINTS.

In this Chapter there will be a considerable amount of repetition, since I shall begin by summing up a few of the most important suggestions in the previous Chapters.

1. During the game keep on the alert before and after every stroke; *be on your toes, ready to move into either position and thence to any spot.*

2. Keep your racket in the Hand-mirror position before and after every stroke.

3. These are two golden rules, and a third is to keep your eye so that it just takes in your opponent, and enables you to judge of the direction of his stroke, until he has made the stroke; then keep your eye fixed on the ball before every stroke, up to the last possible moment.

4. A fourth rule is to *get into position (Forehand or Backhand) the moment you have judged to which side the ball will come.* Start early and, if necessary, move to the ball in this position (either in a few strides or with

GENERAL HINTS

many short steps), so as to be already in position before the ball comes.

5. These movements should be made automatic and instinctive, as far as they can be made so. So should the downward sweep of the racket and the swing of the body on its hips; and so should the upward return of the racket after following through the stroke, and the return to the alert position on the toes.

We said just now that the player must *start early:* the words must be applied in another sense. He or she must start to learn before the body and its muscles and bones are " set ". Children should be drilled in certain movements, with singing or humming, and then they will already have elements ready-made: later on, when they come to play the game, or any new game such as Lawn-Tennis or Golf, they will just have to re-combine these ready-made elements and to add a few special movements. Among them must be mentioned especially the body-swing on the hips (Chap. VIII.).

But I believe it is never too late to begin to learn these movements, whatever may be asserted to the contrary. On insecure foundations no one can build up a sound strong game. Those who naturally have not secure foundations must either lay their foundations anew with labour, or else be content with a low place. The pleasure of improving is so great, that I urge the reader not to grudge the labour, which will not last for long.

But how can the learner tell what is correct? Photos of players, observation of experts, and analyses of their movements, these are the great helps. In observing an expert, do not observe his whole play, but only some one part of it at a time, e. g. his feet, his grip, his wrist. Analyse his positions and movements.

It is very likely that by this means the learner will be able to correct my few suggestions and to add others of his own making, and others made by those who have studied the game. Discussions of various points are well worth starting.

Another famous way of learning is for the learner to try to teach others, especially ladies, until his ideas become definite and logical.

He will probably be able to devise Special Exercises for the various parts of the body, e. g. with the Ball-game Apparatus. These he should note down in a note-book, and practise in addition to the Exercises suggested in these pages. A few Exercises before a game will be a great help.

Above all, do not let him despise Squash, but rather let him learn it thoroughly before he proceeds to Tennis (Court-Tennis) or Racquets. Few have listened to this advice,

GENERAL HINTS 109

but all who have done so have told me that it was perfectly right, i. e that Tennis and Racquets were not the best games for learning Tennis and Racquet, at the outset.

When the commonest strokes of Squash have been mastered, when you can keep the ball down the Side-wall 10 or 15 times, and when you know the various angles, then, I should say, by all means learn these new Games, if you can afford them. But still keep up your Squash; if you are a business-man, play it in the evenings after work.

For the game is worth the electric light: it deserves Championship Matches, if only because of the large number of players who like Squash; and the generosity of those who offered the Cup for the American Amateur Championship, to be played for at the Tuxedo Courts, is much to be praised.

Other Matches should be arranged within Clubs and between Clubs, and records should be kept in Match-books. A well-bound Match-book, with printed headings on each page (Date, Conditions, and Results), helps to preserve the interest.

The Philadelphia Racquet Club has an excellent system of Monthly Handicaps at Racquets, and this is a good idea for Squash. Inter-School and Inter-University Matches, Matches between Schools or Universities and various Clubs, and other Competitions, may raise the standard of the game and may serve as a powerful social influence.

But do not be led by too much Match-play to neglect the practice by which you may strengthen your weak points: if you *must* have a game, then have a Handicap game as often as you can, and practise Exercises at intervals of work, and in the early morning and late at night, when you are not likely to have much to do but yet may not be able to find an opponent.

If you get "stale", then either play with your left hand, or play Fives (Hand-Fives), or take to some other exercise for a time, e. g. to boxing, fencing, walking, running, alternate walking and running, rowing, and riding. Some of these will give you open air, as well as a change.

Staleness seems to me to be a sign that there is something wrong with the system of training; staleness and bad training are such common causes of failure, that a few words on *Training* will not be out of place. The subject has been more fully treated in "The Training of the Body" (Sonnenschein and Co.).

Fresh air is important, as we have recently begun to realise in England. America is behind England here: most rooms and travelling carriages in the winter are execrably venti-

GENERAL HINTS

lated. At present this evil can hardly be escaped by the individual, and to make up for it the window should be opened a little, top and bottom, in the bedroom; and in the early morning it should be opened wide, and the Exercises should be practised after all clothing has been removed. The air-bath and light-bath are invaluable.

As to light, never strain your eyes by bad light or bad print.

In the summer a sun-bath is good: it combines not only air and light but also heat.

Heat, however, is most conveniently obtained from hot water. A *very* hot bath is invigorating, as the Japanese and others have found out long ago. But after a rather hot or a warm bath there should always be cool or cold water (a sponging or a shower or a plunge), followed by vigorous rubbing and exercise.

Cold water is good if you can stand it, but it is seldom good after a meal or when you are either cold or tired. Alternate hot and cold, or warm and cool baths are healthy, especially for the feet the first thing in the morning and the last thing at night.

These have helped many to get to sleep, by drawing the blood downwards from the brain. Sleep is all-important for health and training, and, if you have any difficulty in getting to sleep, then do not work just before going to bed, but take a short walk, and either drink hot or cold water or else eat an apple. I sometimes get to sleep by imagining a game of Racquets or Tennis!

Of Exercise we have said enough already. Boxing improves the alertness and quick movement of the body. Fencing helps the wrist and the weight-shifting, and running helps the wind. The Swedish Gymnastics are to be recommended, and especially the exercise of taking a deep breath upwards through the nose, and then holding it a little time before letting it out again slowly.

Do not neglect left-hand exercises, and, in case you have poor circulation, learn how to massage yourself, since this warms both the hands and the body. The Massage-rollers of the Health Culture Company (503 Fifth Avenue, New York) are a capital idea.

For Squash, avoid Muscle-developers of the ordinary kind. For Squash you do not need huge muscles, but rather that which huge muscles often actually prevent, viz. speed, supple litheness, and promptitude.

These qualities can be helped by Diet: by Diet, fat can be easily and safely removed, and a good state of physical training can be combined with a readiness for mental work: at least this has been my own experience, as I

GENERAL HINTS

have shown elsewhere.* Milk proteid has formed the basis of my food for years, and I have never been out of training for a single day. See Recommendations (under "Biscuits").

---

* In "Muscle, Brain and Diet." (Sonnenschein & Macmillan.)

SPECIFICATION FOR A SQUASH COURT.

BY JAMES B. LORD, ESQ., FIFTH AVENUE, NEW YORK.

The building is to rest on 10 in. locust posts, about six feet apart, and set in the ground below frost line.

The plate on top of posts to be 6in. x 8in. spruce, top plate 3in. x 4in. spruce. Roof 2in. x 8in., 20in. on centers. Main floor beams 3in.x 10in. spruce, 12in. on centers. The main walls of the building to be of 2in. x 4in. studs, 16in. on centres, well braced and cross-bridged.

The outside of the building, including the roof, is to be covered with sawn pine shingles, laid 5½in. to the weather.

All shingles for both side-walls and roof to be laid on shingle strips. The entire inside face of building to be covered with ⅜in. x 2½in. white pine, including the underside of roof rafters.

The flooring is to be ⅜in. x 2½in. T. & G. maple laid on top of ⅜in. rough flooring with two layers of building paper between same.

All doors and sash (including the casing to same) are to be of white pine.

GENERAL HINTS

Skylight of main roof to be constructed of wood, glazed with heavy skylight wire glass, so arranged that every third light is to open by means of approved ratchet rod and wheel.

The windows in the upper part of the court to be hinged at top and to swing out, and so arranged as to be opened easily with approved hardware attachments.

The division between the court proper and the seats is to be constructed of wood, faced on both sides same as side-walls of court, two end pieces to be carried up 12ft. high, in one corner of which furnish and set a flush batten door. The remaining portion of this partition is to be filled in with galvanized iron wire netting.

The seats, lockers, ladder to space over dressing-room, water-closet and shower partitions, and all doors to same are to be of white pine.

Furnish and set one all-porcelain washout closet, trap above floor with tank, lead flush pipes and water connections. The walls of shower to be lined with slate 6ft. high. The shower to be a single overhead sprinkler with approved pull attachment. The floor of shower to be of slate with center drainage.

The plumbing for the water-closet and shower to be carried out 15ft. outside of building, where it will be taken care of by other parties.

Paint all woodwork, excepting shingles, both inside and out, three coats best white lead and oil.

Furnish all necessary hardware and glass.

SQUASH-BOOK

ADVERTISEMENTS

CONTRACTORS...

> The design and specification, kindly devised for the Author by Mr. James Brown Lord, of Fifth Avenue, New York, have received estimates from the following Contractors. The estimates range from under $3,000 to $2,000 (or, without Dressing-room, Plunge-bath, etc., to about $500 less).

Messrs. MEAD & TAFT.
 Cornwall Landing, N. J.

Messrs. MERTZ'S SONS,
 Port Chester, N. Y.

Messrs. VASSAR'S SONS,
 (Builders of the Tuxedo Squash Courts).
 Fifth Avenue, New York.

Advertisements

BOOKS BY THE SAME AUTHOR...

To be obtained from
   Mr. F. E. GRANT,
   23 West 42nd Street, New York.

Lessons in Lawn Tennis. 50 cents

An invaluable help.—*Bristol Athletic News.*

Muscle, Brain, and Diet: A Plea For Simpler Foods. $1.00.

A remarkable book. Mr. Miles makes out probably the best case, for a kind of vegetarianism, that has ever been stated.—*Longman's Magazine.*

With arguments which perforce appeal to the reader as being honest, manly, and scholarly.—*St. James' Gazette.*

How To Prepare Essays, Lectures, Articles, Books, Speeches, and Letters. $2.00.

It is crammed with useful hints.—*Oxford Magazine.*

The work teems with useful suggestions.—*Educational Times.*

The Teaching of Jesus To-Day. $1.00

Mr. Miles has produced a dignified, modern, and intensely powerful version of the Sermon on the Mount.—*Public School Magazine.*

How To Learn Philology. $1.50.

A book of real practical utility.—*Glasgow Herald.*

Advertisements

Mr. Miles approaches the subject with the genius of a born teacher. The book is clear, accurate, thorough, and up-to-date.—*University Correspondent.*

The Training Of The Body.

(In the Press: Sonneschein.)

How To Remember.

(In the Press: Warne & Co.)

A History Of Rome Up To A. D. 500, With Essays.

(In the Press: Grant Richards.)

Recommendations in Alphabetical Order

All the goods mentioned in the following list (up to the pages headed "Advertisements") are personally recommended by the Author.

APPARATUS FOR LEARNING BALL-GAMES (Miles' Patent)...

   For various games.

> Messrs. WRIGHT & DITSON,
> Washington Street, Boston, Mass.

BAGS...

   The Tennis and Racquet Bag.

> This Bag will hold several Court-Tennis or Lawn Tennis or Racquet or Squash Bats, in a Press, together with Flannels, and Evening Clothes, etc.
>
> In it is a list of things usually required during a visit, so that the player will not forget any requisite.

Price complete, with lock and with side straps or fastenings, $25.00.

> Messrs. HAMILTON & CO.,
> 23rd Street and Sixth Avenue, New York.

BALL-GAME EXERCISER AND SELF-TEACHER (Miles' Patent)...

   For various games.

> Messrs. WRIGHT & DITSON,
> Washington Street, Boston, Mass.

BALLS....

   Court-Tennis.

> Messrs. WRIGHT & DITSON, Washington Street, Boston, Mass.
>
> Mr. TOM PETTITT, Boston Athletic Association, Boston, Mass.

Recommendations

Fives.
>Messrs. PROSSER, Pentonville Road, London.

Lawn Tennis.
>Messrs. WRIGHT & DITSON, Washington Street, Boston, Mass.
>Messrs. SLAZENGER, E. 15th Street, New York.

Racquets.
>Messrs. PROSSER, Pentonville Road, London.

Squash-Racquets.
>Messrs. PROSSER, Pentonville Road, London.

Squash-Tennis.
>Messrs. WRIGHT & DITSON, Washington Street, Boston, Mass.
>The *lasting* ball (with special cover), from Wright & Ditson, is very economical.
>Messrs. SLAZENGER, E. 15th Street, New York.

BATS...
>See RACKETS.

BICKLEY CEMENT...
>See CEMENT.

BISCUITS...
>See FOOD.

BOOTS...
>See SHOES.

CARDS, FOR MEMORANDA, ETC. (With Card-Holder)...
Messrs. J. McHUGH,
42nd Street and Fifth Avenue, New York.

CEMENT...
For the best Court-Tennis, Racquet, Squash-Racquet and Squash-Tennis Courts.
Messrs. BICKLEY, Lillie Road, West Brompton, London.

The Bickley Cement has been used for the Tuxedo Court-Tennis Court, where everyone pronounces it a perfect success. The whole Court is uniform—viz. the floor, the back-walls, and the side-walls. The Author has found it to give far the best surface for play at all games, including Racquets, Squash-Tennis, and Squash-Racquets. The Racquet Court at Tuxedo will also be cemented with this Cement. Most of the best Courts in England are cemented by Bickley, who guarantees his work.

CLOTHES...
See FLANNELS.

CONTRACTORS...
Messrs. VASSAR'S SONS,
Fifth Avenue, New York.
And see above.

COURT-TENNIS...
Balls.
Messrs. WRIGHT & DITSON, Washington Street, Boston, Mass.

TOM PETTITT, Boston Athletic Association, Boston, Mass.

Courts.

Messrs. VASSAR'S SONS, Fifth Avenue, New York, constructed the Tuxedo Court. Bickley's Cement was used. Bickley's stain is better than paint for Courts that are already built.

Rackets.

Messrs. NUSSER & CO., 46 Gerrard Street, London, W.

The Author uses Nusser's Court-Tennis Rackets not only in his important Matches, but also for practice for Court-Tennis in a Squash-Court with a Lawn-Tennis ball.

Boots. See SHOES.

COURTS...

See CONTRACTORS. Cement-Courts should never be painted, for the paint as it were chokes the pores of the Court's skin. Bickley's stain has been most successful in England, *e. g.*, at Brighton.

CUPS...

Cups, etc., for Prizes, Messrs. MUNSEY. Market Place, Cambridge, England.

EXERCISER AND SELF-TEACHER FOR * * BALL-GAMES (Miles' Patent)...

For all these games.

Messrs. WRIGHT & DITSON, Washington Street, Boston, Mass.

Recommendations

FIVES....

Balls and Gloves.
>Messrs. PROSSER,
>Pentonville Road, London.

FLANNELS AND CLOTHES...

For all the games.
>Messrs. WRIGHT & DITSON,
>Boston, Mass.

FOOD...

Milk-Proteid Biscuits, with various flavours.
THE DAIRY IMPROVEMENT COMPANY,
>74 John Street, New York.

These Biscuits are more nourishing and sustaining than beef, being richer in proteid or albumen (which is essential to life, since it forms our blood and tissues.) They are compact, palatable, easily digestible, and practically imperishable, being formed of dried (sterilized) milk, without its butter or sugar. They are also the cheapest food known. The Author has found them excellent for training purposes, as they enable him to train without giving up severe brain-work.

They will be ready before Jan. 1. 1901.

HAND-FIVES...

See Fives.

MEMORANDA...

Cards, With Card-Holder.
>Messrs. J. McHUGH,
>42nd Street, New York.

Recommendations

NOTES...
    See CARDS.

PLASTER...
    For sore hands, blisters, etc.
        JOHNSON'S ADHESIVE PLASTER
            From all Chemists.

PRIZES...
    See CUPS.

RACKETS...
    Court-Tennis.
        Messrs. NUSSER & CO., 46 Gerrard Street, London.
        See, also, under COURT-TENNIS.

    Lawn Tennis.
        Messrs. WRIGHT & DITSON, Washington Street, Boston, Mass.
        Messrs. SLAZENGER, E. 15th Street, New York.

    Racquets.
        Messrs. PROSSER, Pentonville Road, London.

    Squash-Racquets
        Messrs. PROSSER, Pentonville Road, London.

    .Squash-Tennis.
        Messrs. WRIGHT & DITSON, Washington Street, Boston, Mass.
        For the Larned Racket see Chapter I.
        Messrs. SLAZENGER, E. 15th Street, New York.

Recommendations 131

RACQUETS...
 Balls.
  Messrs. PROSSER, Pentonville Road, London.

SHOES...
 For all the games.
  NEWMAN, the Shoeman,
  Tremont Building, Harvard Square,
  Boston, Mass.

SQUASH...
 Balls.
  See BALLS.
 Bats.
  See RACKETS.
 Courts.
  See CONTRACTORS, and CEMENT.
 Rackets.
  See RACKETS.
 Shoes.
  See SHOES.

TENNIS...
 See COURT-TENNIS, LAWN TENNIS.

CENTRAL COLLECTION

ADVERTISEMENTS

Messrs. BICKLEY

Lillie Road
West Brompton
London

Bickley's Cement

and

Bickley's Stain.....

for

 Court-Tennis..
Racquet and..
Squash Courts

(See recommendations)

ADVERTISEMENTS

Dairy Improvement Co.

74 JOHN STREET

NEW YORK

...MILK-PROTEID...
BISCUITS

(To be ready by January 1, 1901)

PLEASANT

    DIGESTIBLE

        NOURISHING

            PURE

                CHEAP

See recommendations.

ADVERTISEMENTS

Messrs. HAMILTON, 23d Street and Sixth Avenue, New York.

The Greatest "Trunk Corner" in America

HAMILTON'S
LEATHER GOODS
════AND TRUNKS

S. E. Cor. 23d St. and Sixth Ave.

Telephone 2888–18th St.   NEW YORK

EUROPEAN OUTFITS

THE TENNIS AND RACQUET AND SQUASH-TENNIS BAG

BAGS OF VARIOUS KINDS

ADVERTISEMENTS

NEWMAN...

The Shoeman

TREMONT BUILDING
HARVARD SQUARE
CAMBRIDGE, MASS.

Athletic Shoes for Men and Women

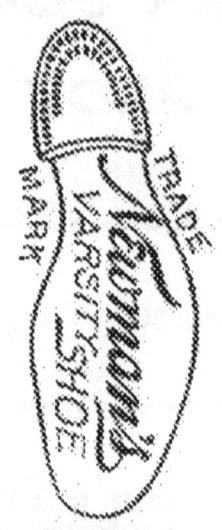

STREET AND DRESS SHOES

CATALOGUES SENT FREE

ADVERTISEMENTS

Messrs. NUSSER

46 GERRARD STREET

LONDON

Manufacturers of

Rackets for Court-Tennis

(See Recommendations)

Lawn Tennis Racquets

Squash Racquets

AND OF IMPLEMENTS
FOR THESE GAMES.

ADVERTISEMENTS

Messrs. PROSSER

PENTONVILLE ROAD

LONDON

Makers of all sorts of materials for

Cricket
Football
Hockey
Racquets
Squash-Racquets
Fives

AND OTHER GAMES

ADVERTISEMENTS

Messrs. SLAZENGER

5 and 7 E. 15th Street

NEW YORK

LAWN TENNIS
   SQUASH-TENNIS
      RACQUETS
         TENNIS
            POLO

GOLF
   CRICKET
      LAWN BOWLS
         HOCKEY
            CROQUET
               CURLING

Complete outfit for above games

ADVERTISEMENTS

GEORGE VASSAR'S SON & CO.

111 FIFTH AVENUE
NEW YORK

Contractors for Courts for

SQUASH-TENNIS

RACQUETS and

COURT-TENNIS

Builders of the Tuxedo Court-Tennis and . . . Squash-Tennis Courts

(See Recommendations)

ADVERTISEMENTS

Messrs. WRIGHT & DITSON
Washington Street, Boston, Mass.

WRIGHT & DITSON

"Squash" Tennis Ba

**Headquarters for everything pertaining to
SQUASH-TENNIS and
LAWN TENNIS GOODS**

Ball-Game Exerciser (Miles' Patent) for various Games.

The Squash-Tennis Ball is made of the finest rubber cloth, covered and sewed, Per Doz. $4.00
Special all-Rubber ball .... Per Doz. $3.00
Wright & Ditson Squash-Tennis Rackets, strung with fine quality gut .... each, $2.50

www.ingramcontent.com/pod-product-compliance
Lightning Source LLC
Chambersburg PA
CBHW031254230426
43670CB00005B/175